Contemporary Studies in Literature

Eugene Ehrlich, *Columbia University*
Daniel Murphy, *City University of New York*
Series Editors

Volumes include:

William Faulkner

a collection of criticism edited by Dean Morgan Schmitter

McGraw-Hill Book Company

New York · St. Louis · San Francisco · London · Düsseldorf
Kuala Lumpur · Mexico · Montreal · Panama · Rio de Janeiro
Sydney · Toronto · Johannesburg · New Delhi · Singapore

23456789MUMU79876543

Library of Congress Cataloging in Publication Data

Schmitter, Dean M.   comp.
  William Faulkner.

  (Contemporary studies in literature)
  Bibliography: p.
  1. Faulkner, William, 1897–1962.
PS3511.A86Z966   813'.5'2   72-7739
ISBN 0-07-055387-4

Preface

The richness of Faulkner's work and the complexity resulting from continued use of the same characters and incidents have combined to make Faulkner a writer who especially needs explanation. As a result, his work has called forth a considerable body of critical literature, some of it designed simply to keep characters and incidents straight. Four books, for instance, have been published that are essentially indexes to the novels and stories. Three more books present the kind of basic information designed to guide readers through the fiction. Dozens of other books and hundreds of articles contribute both factual information and broad critical interpretations.

The selection of material for the present volume has been planned to assist readers and students who feel the need for basic critical assistance in appreciating Faulkner's major work and gaining an introduction to the scope of his accomplishment. Although the aim has not been to give a cross section of the criticism or to sample its variety, some such effect is inevitable. The selections in Part I discuss general characteristics and problems, and those in Part II concentrate on the six novels most likely to be read. The Bibliography, after listing the books written by Faulkner, is limited with two exceptions to books about him or his work, under the belief that a selection from the hundreds of articles and essays would not be readily available to most readers. For the reader who wants to investigate the criticism further, help will be found in the Bibliography under the subsection "Of Works about Faulkner."

D. M. S.

Columbia University, January 1973

Contents

Dean Morgan Schmitter

Introduction: The Faulkner Legend

"I am a farmer, a country man and I like to write. . . . I like horses—I breed and train horses. That is what I like to do more than writing,"[1] William Faulkner told a Japanese audience, repeating a remark that in one form or another has amused or frustrated his readers for over forty years. But regardless of the order in which he ranked his pleasures, he was first of all a writer and, in our current opinion, one of America's greatest.

Of all American authors he has remained most true to his local roots and not grafted himself onto others. It is true, of course, that many novelists have found it advantageous to set their work in places and among people they knew well. In much the same way that Milton used the familiar materials of Christian and classical myth, Hemingway used the actual Michigan and Spanish and Caribbean areas that he knew. But no writer anywhere has ever made a more striking use of the area that nurtured him than has Faulkner. Nor has any writer been more successful in forcing the dusty details of the real world that he knew to tell tales of the human heart and spirit.

The most important quality of Faulkner's work is undoubtedly the blaze of genius whose genesis we do not know and have not the means to uncover. Immediately apparent is the fact that he was a Southerner whose mode of expression was shaped by the habits of northern Mississippi, not simply by the daily routine but by its hopes and fears for the present, the future, and the past—especially the past. Fed through Faulkner's imagination, the Southern heritage grew into a fiction that presented familiar faces and voices to his neighbors, but intensified them into unfamiliar and disturbing experiences. There were non-Southerners, however, who eagerly accepted the narratives as factual accounts of the grotesquery and corruption they expected from Southern decadence. The novelist himself had not chosen either to describe or expose his homeland, but only to tell stories using the characteristics of people and places he knew, or as a younger novelist has remarked

[1] *Faulkner at Nagano,* ed. Robert A Jelliffe (Tokyo: Kenkyusha, 1956), p. 194.

1

about his own subject matter, it was "by predetermination, his meat."[2]

Faulkner's meat, of course, was the area where he had been reared: Oxford, Mississippi, and the surrounding countryside. It furnished the setting for his fiction, which he called Yoknapatawpha County with its county seat, Jefferson; there he settled the characters and incidents for his major work. The relationship of Yoknapatawpha and Jefferson with his home county, Lafayette, and the actual Oxford has intrigued his audience for two reasons: first, factual similarity provides a puzzle for the curious reader and, for the serious one, a thought-provoking look into the alchemy of an artist; and, second, no other writer has created such a unified body of work by extending a single provincial spot with its set of characters through so many novels and short stories. His faithfulness to his source material, however, is about what we might expect from a creative writer; he used it in any way he pleased to bring his characters to life.

It is so easy to be carried away with the vividness of this "little postage stamp of earth," as Faulkner called it, that we may forget that it was indeed only a "tool," as he also called it, a way of creating the successes and failures of imaginary characters who have been caught up and tossed about in imaginary events. The writer, Faulkner told students at the University of Virginia with obvious reference to himself, "is writing about people in the terms he's most familiar with. . . . He is using the material which he knows, the tools which are at hand."[3] Faulkner had never thought that he was merely a Southern writer, or that the ultimate aim of his work was to depict a regional consciousness and legend. He had gently pointed out to Malcolm Cowley in 1944 that the Southern material was merely his peephole on the human situation.

> I'm inclined to think that my material, the South, is not very important to me. I just happen to know it, and don't have time in one life to learn another one and write at the same time. Though the one I know is probably as good as another, life is a phenomenon but not a novelty, the same frantic steeplechase toward nothing everywhere and man stinks the same no matter where in time.[4]

[2] John Updike in a facetious article printed in the *New York Times Book Review* called "'Henry Bech Redux' by Henry Bech," Nov. 14, 1971, p. 3.

[3] *Faulkner in the University,* ed. Frederick L. Gwynn and Joseph L. Blotner (New York: Vintage Books, 1959), p. 57.

[4] Quoted in Malcolm Cowley, *The Faulkner-Cowley File* (New York: Viking Press, 1966), pp. 14–15.

This observation has been critically important and was soon put in the record by Robert Penn Warren's declaration that Faulkner's work should be regarded "in terms of issues which are common to our modern world. The legend is not merely a legend of the South, but is also a legend of our general plight and problem."[5]

But it was still the Southern locale, "the background, the color, the smells, the sounds," all of which included the South of legend as well as the South of his boyhood, that led him to the general plight and problem of humanity. For it was Faulkner's fortune to have been born and reared in a section of the country that had a history and a myth as no other did.

Part of this history was Faulkner's own great-grandfather, an extraordinary figure who had played a part in the period that gave Southerners their most poignant memory. Colonel William Clark Falkner[6] had gained his military title during the Civil War, and he had also practiced law, built a railroad, written a popular novel, and died a violent death, shot by a former partner. His career was, indeed, of the stuff that families remember, and his great-grandson heard the stories throughout his early years, finally memorializing him in his third novel, *Sartoris,* as the model for Colonel John Sartoris.

The two generations of Falkners that followed the Colonel lived in quieter times and led quieter lives. Respectable and responsible citizens, they filled their places in the community with honor and no doubt passed on to their grandson and son the sense of belonging that he must have had. For the attitude that Faulkner brought to his provincial setting is rare for an American, issuing from such assurance of his rightful place in the society that he needed neither to defend nor attack it but only to possess it with a kind of proprietory right. Family continuity certainly contributed to the sense of simultaneous attachment and detachment that he expressed in the essay "Mississippi": "Home again, his native land; he was born of it and his bones will sleep in it; loving it even while hating some of it," and, like a chorus, reiterating a few pages later, "Loving all of it even while he had to hate some of it because he knows now that you don't love because: you love despite; not for

---

[5] Review of *The Portable Faulkner,* in *William Faulkner: Three Decades of Criticism,* ed. Frederick J. Hoffman and Olga W. Vickery (New York: Harcourt, Brace, 1963), p. 112.

[6] The common spelling, with a *u,* was accepted by Faulkner and appears on all his books. He professed not to know how the change occurred, nor to care one way or the other.

the virtues, but despite the faults."[7] Whatever personal fissures reft Faulkner's soul, they were not those of a man without a country; he knew well that he was a fourth-generation Mississippian, and he must have been reared to believe that "all the Falkners are honorable people,"[8] as his fellow townsman John Cullen said. With such assurance one can be eccentric without considering the means.

If Faulkner's social inheritance is to be called aristocratic, it is aristocratic only in a limited sense, that of a rural or small-town setting where social lines are movable and blurred at the edges. Honorable forebears could be a distinct advantage, but they were not all. Murry Falkner, William's father, had a head start toward respectability, but he was not born to position. With his own father, John Wesley Thompson Falkner, called by courtesy the "young Colonel" as president of the family railroad, Murry Falkner had worked at various positions, being a general passenger agent when his first son, William, was born in 1897. When William was five, and with two younger sons—Murry, Jr., three, and John, one—he moved to Oxford, where he spent the remainder of his life, moving from one modest business venture to another until he finally became secretary and business manager at the University of Mississippi. The youngest son, Dean, later killed in an airplane crash, was born in Oxford.

There the family lived close by the "young Colonel," and there William was to go through his boyhood and young manhood, to hold various jobs, to marry and become a father, to attain world fame, and finally to die and be buried. Stories about him have been printed and passed by word of mouth, scores of stories with a peculiar consistency that has created a legend, but the truth is that we know little about his private life and less about his inner self.[9]

The boyhood, as we read about it from his brothers John and Murry and from the anecdotes of friends and neighbors, has the idyllic glow of life at the turn of the century in a small town, comfortable and secure in the midst of family and friends, with ponies and dogs and chickens, with the pranks and games and escapades that filled the lives of thousands and thousands of his contemporaries. The difference lay in the local color of Southern life:

[7] In *Essays, Speeches, and Public Letters,* ed. James B. Meriwether (New York: Random House, 1965), pp. 36, 43.

[8] John B. Cullen, *Old Times in the Faulkner Country* (Chapel Hill: University of North Carolina Press, 1961), p. 7.

[9] Joseph L. Blotner has been named the official biographer by Faulkner's family.

an aunt—"Auntee" the Falkner boys called her—whose single swear word was *damn* as a prefix to *Yankee;* a "mammy," tiny Callie Barr with her snuff stick and starched dress and apron, who fussed over the Falkner boys with such devotion that she now graces the dedication page to *Go Down, Moses:* "To Mammy, Caroline Barr, Mississippi (1840–1940), who was born in slavery and who gave to my family a fidelity without stint or calculation of recompense and to my childhood an immeasurable devotion and love." Brother Murry Falkner tells also of their grandmother, who, indignant at plans to place the monument to the Confederate soldier north of the courthouse, insisted it should be on the *south* side, and prevailed.[10]

The known accounts tell us nothing of the deeper conflicts and forces within Faulkner during these early years. Perhaps they were as normal as they seem, but it is difficult to believe so. Edmond L. Volpe's study of Faulkner has convinced him that the formative years must have been torn with spiritual and psychological turbulence.[11] There has to be an explanation somewhere for the persistent stories, too many and too similar to ignore, about Faulkner's drinking habits, which far exceeded the traditional love of bourbon. There seems little doubt that as much as this strong-willed Southerner controlled his own life, he could not always control his drinking and at intervals drank to such excess that he was incapacitated for extended periods. Typically, about all he ever said publicly was that drinking was "a normal and healthy instinct" and left the world to think as it would. But whatever the causes, whatever fears and guilts he allowed liquor to blot out, he did not allow it to cut him off from a productive life of extraordinary achievement.

Around Faulkner during his early years, of course, was the Southern mixture of violence and courtliness, of frontier readiness and cavalier aspirations. He heard much of the past, especially the Civil War, in the stories of family and neighbors: "I never read any history," he said in 1938. "I talked to people around who had lived through it, and I would pick it up—I was just saturated with it but never read about it."[12] He learned to know the country people around Oxford in much the same way. John Faulkner

[10] *The Falkners of Mississippi* (Baton Rouge: Louisiana State University Press, 1967), pp. 29–30.

[11] *A Reader's Guide to William Faulkner* (New York: Farrar, Straus, 1964), p. 5.

[12] Quoted in Robert Cantwell, "The Faulkners: Recollections of a Gifted Family," in Hoffman and Vickery (eds.), *William Faulkner: Three Decades,* p. 57.

records one period in his brother's life during which he attended many country dances, "watching and listening" and occasionally dipping into a tub of whiskey. [13]

Faulkner was a notably independent man, and the sign of it was in the wind early. After two years of high school, "he just sort of quit," as his brother John remembered it, and his parents, recognizing his mettle, gave in to the inevitable. Except for a brief period as a special student at the University of Mississippi after the First World War, he had concluded his formal education. Fortunately, he came to the attention of Phil Stone, a graduate of Yale and later a lawyer in Oxford, who recognized his young friend's talent and set him on a course of reading that was carefully and well selected. In a big Studebaker touring car loaned to him by the Stones, Faulkner would set out with a load of books to spend the day reading on a quiet country road. [14]

With his first novel still some ten years away, the nineteen-year-old Faulkner first worked as a bookkeeper in his grandfather's bank. Then, disappointed at several attempts to enlist for war service, he maneuvered his way into the Royal Air Force flight training program. In July 1918 he departed for Canada to begin training, but the Armistice cut short his military career and by December he had returned to Oxford to live with his family, becoming in 1921 the postmaster at the University, where his father had a house on the campus.

His few months in the military and his few years in the postmastership have both performed more than their share of service in providing stories for the Faulkner legend. For years biographical accounts credited Faulkner with shooting down one or two planes in France, and sometimes with a romantically near-fatal crash. It is doubtful that Faulkner started the stories, but it is certain that he made only indirect attempts to correct them. Perhaps he enjoyed the garbled accounts, a view not inconsistent with Malcolm Cowley's belief that he was following "his fixed principle of never correcting misstatements about himself." [15]

It is not likely that Faulkner as postmaster actually threw the mail in the garbage can as he said he was accused of doing, but there were many observers who have come forward to testify along with Phil Stone that "he made the damndest postmaster the World

[13] *My Brother Bill,* (New York: Pocket Books, 1964), p. 143.
[14] Ibid., pp. 115–16.
[15] See Cowley, *The Faulkner-Cowley File,* pp. 71–75.

has ever seen."[16] His performance, which seemed to consist of reading and writing in preference to delivering letters and packages and selling stamps, is matched only by that of the postal authorities who let him stay on for almost three years, until October 1924, when the complaints had risen to such a pitch that the unwilling civil servant chose to resign rather than mend his ways, maintaining in his first memorable quotation that he "didn't intend to be beholden to every son of a bitch who had two cents to buy a stamp."[17]

His postmastership gave him no material for writing, but his few months as a fledgling pilot did; his first short story, "Landing in Luck," published by the University newspaper, *The Mississippian,* in 1919, makes use of his Canadian experience. Even before that, *The New Republic* had published a poem called "L'Apres-Midi d'un Faune." These minor accomplishments indicate Faulkner's early intentions toward writing, or perhaps toward artistic expression, for he had already published drawings in the University annual. During the time he was close to the University, the publications there had given space to his drawings, poems, and both fiction and nonfiction. Encouraged by Stone, Faulkner seems to have considered himself mainly a poet, an ambition that was to culminate by 1933 in two volumes of verse, including his first published volume, *The Marble Faun* (1924). Students of his work have since remarked on the poetic quality of his fiction, presumably meaning the emotional intensity. Faulkner's stated desire to get all his meaning into one sentence, to epitomize experience, is indeed the mark of the poet. Except for its fluency and occasional rhetorical flashes, the early poetry shows little of the direction his talent was to follow in the sweeping prose of his maturity, but he was always to refer to himself as a "spoiled poet," never to succeed in capturing the precise expression he sought, but to try and try again.

The first novel, *Soldier's Pay* (1926), was written in New Orleans, where he had met and taken a liking to Sherwood Anderson, whose easy life, he humorously declared, persuaded him to become a novelist. Faulkner had stopped in New Orleans on his way to Europe but stayed on, intrigued by the literary atmosphere and

---

[16] Quoted in Michael Millgate, *The Achievement of William Faulkner* (New York: Random House, 1966), p. 10. The 57-page opening chapter of this book is currently the most extensive, dependable biography of Faulkner available.

[17] John Faulkner, *My Brother Bill,* p. 128.

submitting material to New Orleans publications.[18] He then carried out his plans to visit Europe, returning after six months and soon completing his second apprentice novel, *Mosquitoes* (1927).

The future Nobel Prize winner had found his vocation but not his proper subject matter, although that was not long in coming. Even before *Mosquitoes* was published, he set to work on a story of "the aristocratic, chivalrous and ill-fated Sartoris family," thus beginning the fictional history of Yoknapatawpha County. The creation began close to home, with the "old Colonel," W. C. Falkner, serving as the model for Colonel Sartoris, and there is sufficient reason for believing that further members of the family lent details to other characters. Thirty years later, when his world had become a subject for study, Faulkner advised readers "to begin with a book called *Sartoris* that has the germ of my apocrypha in it. . . . I'd say that's a good one to begin with."[19]

Having discovered his "tools," Faulkner then submerged himself in building one of his most beautiful creations, the four sections of *The Sound and the Fury,* often considered his finest novel. Disappointed by the difficulty of finding a publisher and by the lack of public enthusiasm, he seems to have heeded only the cry within himself in writing the story: "I had just written my guts into *The Sound and the Fury* though I was not aware until the book was published that I had done so, because I had done it for pleasure,"[20] he wrote elsewhere, recalling the most poignant experience of his career. It was his favorite book; he refused to say it was the best, but it was the closest to his heart and the one he felt "tenderest" about.

The way to publication was still not easy, but the creative energy released, apparently by certainty in his own powers, turned the next dozen years into a dazzling record of literary genius: *As I Lay Dying; Sanctuary; Light in August; Absalom, Absalom!; The Hamlet;* and *Go Down, Moses* were only slightly more than half the titles published over Faulkner's name from 1930 to 1942. Except for the reputation *Sanctuary* gained as a novel of sensation, there was still no great public response, and only a few critics and writers paid him much heed. Hemingway is reported to have let

[18] The published material from this period has been collected by Carvel Collins in *William Faulkner: New Orleans Sketches* (New York: Grove Press, 1961). There is a revised edition published by Random House (1968). Mr. Collins has also collected the earlier writing in *William Faulkner: Early Prose and Poetry* (Boston: Little, Brown, 1962).

[19] *Faulkner in the University,* p. 285.

[20] Introduction to *Sanctuary* (New York: Modern Library, 1932), p. vi.

his guard down long enough to declare that Faulkner's talent was of such high order that he would "have been happy just to have managed him." Abroad, especially in France, enthusiasm ran high; for young people in France, Jean Paul Sartre said, Faulkner was a god,[21] although it may be said that appreciation ran several laps ahead of understanding. But in the summer of 1944 Malcolm Cowley assessed the general situation when he wrote to Faulkner, admitting candidly that "in publishing circles your name is mud." Maxwell Perkins, editor for Fitzgerald, Hemingway, and Wolfe, told Cowley a little later that "Faulkner is finished."[22] This depressed period in Faulkner's fortunes has become an episode in the legend, often exaggerated, for the novelist did have admirers, not the least of whom was Cowley himself, starting on a study of the writings that was to result in *The Portable Faulkner* (1946), destined to bring new attention to the completed work. The novelist himself said nothing, quietly going about his business, but he could hardly have escaped discouragement and frustration. Years later he told a Japanese audience, "In my country, an artist is nothing."[23] When he made the statement he was a celebrity—sought out and sung to in ways that would have delighted a person far more hungry for adulation than Faulkner ever seemed to be.

No books were published by Faulkner from 1942 to 1948, but it assuredly was not true that he was finished, either in power or popularity, though many critics have seen the later writings as a decline from the previous work. A difference there is, but only a difference that might have enhanced a lesser reputation. In 1940 Faulkner had told a visitor, "Ten years ago I was much better. Used to take more chances."[24] Much later, he perhaps explained what he meant by taking chances when he mused that an older writer wants to correct his writing and make it clear because he pays more attention to what people think of his work.[25] Certainly Faulkner was busy during this period, partly in Hollywood earning the money that his books had not earned and working away at his own writing when he was free of contractual obligations. After the popular success of *Sanctuary* and until the period of financial security, he used Hollywood to augment his income. Especially hard-pressed for money, he spent part of each year from 1942 to

[21] See Cowley, *The Faulkner-Cowley File,* pp. 29, 24.

[22] Ibid., pp. 9, 10n.

[23] *Faulkner at Nagano,* p. 197.

[24] Quoted in Dan Brennan, "Journey South," in *Lion in the Garden,* ed. James B. Meriwether and Michael Millgate (New York: Random House, 1968), p. 49.

[25] *Faulkner at Nagano,* pp. 153–54, 160.

1945 in the film center, returning when he could to Rowanoak, the antebellum home he had purchased years before in Oxford.

After *Intruder in the Dust* (1948) he published nine more books, and the list ended only with the author's death. His last novel, *The Reivers,* was issued only a month before he died. These same years, especially after 1950, were busy with other activities. With fame thrust upon him, Faulkner shed part of his reticence and accepted his role as a public figure, speaking out as never before, giving interviews, commenting on the integration crisis, representing the United States as a cultural luminary, and accepting the position of Writer-in-Residence at the University of Virginia. His winning of the 1949 Nobel Prize, for which he traveled to Stockholm the following year, was the turning point, of course, and Faulkner, either from choice or from duty, seemed to recognize that his well-worn guise of the farmer who liked to write books could tolerate an added dimension. Public honors multiplied. So did books and critical articles and new printings of his own books, until now he is one of the most read and reverently studied authors on the American scene. Nor has his reputation shown any signs of subsiding in the years since his death.

The foregoing account suggests but does not complete the Faulkner legend, essentially an image of the man through peeps and glimpses, through stories told and retold and exaggerated, and bred from an insatiable curiousity to penetrate the mask, or perhaps the wall, that the writer put up to the public. It is difficult in an era when public figures crowd our vision not to consider high public visibility a fact of nature, especially when we have a whole industry to perform the task. One of the first facts of Faulkner's personality, however, was that he was a private man, forced to work hard at maintaining his privacy, and in so doing unwittingly creating a reputation all the more intriguing for his efforts. Nor should it surprise us that this demeanor was especially attractive to the public; the press sought out stories about the taciturn, pipe-smoking Southerner, whose strong individualism was seasoned with a countryman's oblique humor, a humor not unlike that of one of his most attractive characters, Ratliff in the Snopes trilogy. It is difficult to avoid the suspicion that Faulkner enjoyed part of the game and used it occasionally to satisfy a droll sense of humor, as in his response to an invitation to attend a dinner of notables at the White House: a hundred miles, he drawled, was a long way to go just to eat. The legend satisfies much of our rustic folklore about ourselves: an artist who did not act like an artist, who wired his own house for electricity, who hunted and drank with boyhood companions; a fond father who detoured through Stockholm to receive a prize from the hands of a king so his daughter could see Paris. Thousands of readers have chuckled over his purported refusal to receive a visiting celebrity: no, he said, he had a "previous engagement to hunt a coon."

The attractiveness of the image depends largely on the knowledge that the protagonist meant it. The record shows that Faulkner made a clear distinction between his writing, which he submitted to the public for its use, and his private self, which he did not. Of the former he talked as openly as his nature would allow in the interviews that now serve as valuable adjuncts to the creative writing. A few years earlier he might have been unwilling to project himself so far into the record. In 1949 he wrote to Malcolm Cowley:

> It is my ambition to be, as a private individual, abolished and voided from history, leaving it markless, no refuse save the books; I wish I had had enough sense to see ahead thirty years ago and like some of the Elizabethans, not signed them. It is my aim, and every effort bent, that the sum and history of my life, which in the same sentence is my obit and epitaph too, shall be them both: He made the books and he died.[26]

Faulkner's attempt to live up to this personal invisibility threw him into ambiguous situations and moods, which have left behind contradictory stories of his courtesy and his rudeness. At times he resorted to wildly facetious fancy, as when he told a Memphis reporter that he "was born in 1826 of a negro slave and an alligator,"[27] but he was capable also of coolly, or coldly, ignoring questions and advances. Dignity and courtesy were part of his Southern heritage of good manners, but he could also use these traits to stand off either private or journalistic intrusions. The Keep Out sign that he himself painted and posted at the end of his driveway in Oxford was meant for the merely curious intruder, but impersonal and organized journalistic probing agitated deeper principles and forced the note of helpless anger that rides through an essay he published in 1955.

> The American sky which was once the topless empyrean of freedom, the American air which was once the living breath of liberty, are now become one vast down-crowding pressure to abolish them both, by

[26] Quoted in Cowley, *The Faulkner-Cowley File*, p. 126.
[27] Quoted in Meriwether and Millgate, *Lion in the Garden*, p. 7; see also p. 9.

destroying man's individuality as a man by (in that turn) destroying
the last vestige of privacy without which man cannot be an individual.[28]

As long as he lived, he reserved the right to choose the terms on
which he would expose himself, maintaining the same individuality
with which he carried on his work, ignoring the critics while he
went about his business. Whatever hurts he suffered he endured
in privacy, just as he made himself into an artist in isolation.

Except for the demands that his career as a writer made upon
him, the scant and inconclusive information available suggests
that Faulkner lived a fairly settled personal life in Oxford. Until
the 1950s when he moved about more, he only occasionally traveled to New York or elsewhere, generally on publishing business,
or for longer periods to California to work as a writer for the
motion picture studios. In 1929 he had married Estelle Oldham,
a divorcee with two children, who had once been his teenage
sweetheart. Of their own two daughters, only the younger, Jill,
survived, and it is said that Faulkner went to the University of
Virginia to be near her and his grandchildren. At his death he still
owned a 320-acre farm several miles from Oxford, and Rowanoak,
the columned old house in Oxford that he had partly repaired
himself. His funeral service was conducted there in the parlor, the
coffin before the hearth, surrounded by his family, with close
friends in the adjoining dining room.

Faulkner was over fifty years old before the great body of his
compatriots discovered that their foremost literary figure lived
in a Southern country town, and that lurking behind his bizarre
and driven characters was a strikingly compassionate and traditional view of human moral and spiritual qualities. He had to
create a mode and stake out his own world before many critics
and most readers could shake themselves free of their literary
expectations so expertly served by writers like Hemingway and
Fitzgerald, who dominated the younger generation of American
writers while Faulkner was shaping his quite different art. Faulkner's microcosm, his Yoknapatawpha County, was not from the
first mapped and surveyed, with the literary seismographs noting
every tremor as they have been for the last two decades.

Now we come to his work with the widely disseminated dic-
tum that he is one of America's greatest novelists, fit to rank with

[28] "On Privacy (The American Dream: What happened to it?)," in *Essays,
Speeches, and Public Letters*, p. 72.

Hawthorne, Twain, and James. The uncertain reader may know and tremble at the rule that if he finds Faulkner's work difficult, it is he who is lacking, not the author. Still, there must be many readers who, trying to understand *The Sound and the Fury* for the first time, have their confidence shattered by the effort. Very few readers, and very few critics either, have the assurance to say, as it has been said, that "it is not hard to follow with sufficient accuracy the shifts of time in the Benjy section,"[29] a statement that can be made only after the reader has worked very hard to analyze the section. The knowledge that it is possible to discover the patterns in Faulkner's most difficult writing is many hours away from actual success in finding them, and the effort may still not be rewarded adequately in every passage. The troubled reader will find solace in the admission by one of Faulkner's most sympathetic critics, Cleanth Brooks, that some passages in Quentin's section of *The Sound and the Fury* are "so private as to be almost incomprehensible" and that in *The Hamlet* he "had difficulty in making out precisely what went on in the Flem-Ratliff trade."[30]

Brooks's statements point up two principal ways in which Faulkner's style may throw barriers before his readers. Of the many furies that drove Faulkner in his writing, the most obsessive was the attempt to somehow capture the inchoate sense of complication that makes up the totality of human experience, the sense that every human being is composed of his own presence shaped by history's past, of reason and passion as finely interwoven as a Persian carpet, and, perhaps most important of all, of man's moral being beset by forces within and without, forces that none of his characters can ever quite master. In passages of high tension, Faulkner strove against the impossible to combine such elements in language, not by finding the precise word, like Flaubert, but by a rush of words that cascade and build as though he cannot accumulate enough variations to create the full experience. The resulting rhetoric, though not the only element in Faulkner's style, is the most distinctive, and when pushed to the limit may obscure meaning for the reader, who, if all else fails, may still profit by relaxing and enjoying it.

Another feature of Faulkner's style is the manner in which he releases information, sometimes preventing the reader from having full perspective on what is happening. Although the reader

---

[29] Richard Chase, *The American Novel and Its Tradition* (Garden City, N.Y.: Doubleday, 1957), p. 227.

[30] *William Faulkner: The Yoknapatawpha Country* (New Haven: Yale University Press, 1963), pp. 326, 402n.

accumulates information as he goes along, often he must wait
pages to find the facts he needs, or with *Absalom, Absalom!* until
the end of the novel. For instance, the goat-trading incident in
The Hamlet mentioned by Brooks is presented so obliquely that
the scheming of the characters follows a trail too devious for the
reader to track. One explanation is that the author is so close to
his characters, has imagined them so fully in his own mind, and
follows them from so close a perspective that he seldom steps back
to provide the kind of expository information that we are accus-
tomed to. A case in point occurs in *Go Down, Moses,* in which all
but one of the stories are about the descendants, both black and
white, of L. Q. C. McCaslin. But in "Pantaloon in Black" the main
character is an apparently unrelated Negro workman named
Rider. Asked about the discrepancy, Faulkner calmly replied that
Rider also was a McCaslin descendant.[31] That information, the
connecting link, was nowhere available in the book. Generally,
of course, the details are available, Faulkner having placed them
artfully as the scenes unfold, but the reader must assemble them
in his mind to understand the intricate pattern the author has
created.

Both these traits are simply aspects of Faulkner's style;
though the reader may sometimes stumble over them, they also
add power and intensity to the experience. Much of the prose is
focused sharply on the action and can be, as in the famous short
story, "A Rose for Emily," a model of narrative clarity, even
though the author is too immersed in action and character to
interpret the significance. Where the reader is most likely to wel-
come critical help is in realizing fully what he senses in the action,
the humanistic and spiritual implications that hover over the
printed pages.

---

[31] Quoted in Cowley, *The Faulkner-Cowley File,* p. 113.

Part I   General Criticism

Malcolm Cowley

Yoknapatawpha County:
Faulkner's "Mythical Kingdom"

Faulkner's mythical kingdom is a county in northern Mississippi, on the border between the sand hills covered with scrubby
pine and the black earth of the river bottoms. Except for the store-
keepers, mechanics, and professional men who live in Jefferson,
the county seat, all the inhabitants are farmers or woodsmen.
Except for a little lumber, their only commercial product is baled
cotton for the Memphis market. A few of them live in big plantation houses, the relics of another age, and more of them in
substantial wooden farmhouses; but still more of them are tenants,
no better housed than slaves on good plantations before the Civil
War. Yoknapatawpha County—"William Faulkner, sole owner
and proprietor," as he inscribed on one of the maps he drew—has
a population of 15,611 persons scattered over 2400 square miles.
It sometimes seems to me that every house or hovel has been described in one of Faulkner's novels, and that all the people of the
imaginary county, black and white, townsmen, farmers, and house-
wives, have played their parts in one connected story.

He has so far [1945] written nine books wholly concerned
with Yoknapatawpha County and its people, who also appear in
parts of three others and in thirty or more uncollected stories.
Sartoris was the first of the books to be published, in the spring of
1929; it is a romantic and partly unconvincing novel, but with
many fine scenes in it, such as the hero's visit to a family of
independent pine-hill farmers; and it states most of the themes that
the author would later develop at length. *The Sound and the*

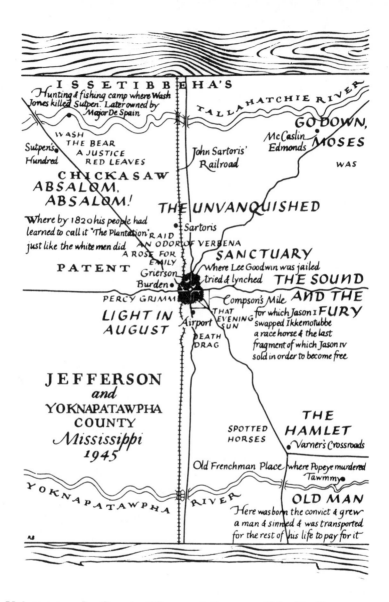

Yoknapatawpha County, "Surveyed & mapped" by Faulkner

Fury, published six months later, recounts the going-to-pieces of the Compson family, and it was the first of Faulkner's novels to be widely discussed. The books that followed, in the Yoknapatawpha series, are *As I Lay Dying* (1930), about the death and burial of Addie Bundren; *Sanctuary* (1931), for a long time the most popular of his novels; *Light in August* (1932), in some ways the best; *Absalom, Absalom!* (1936), about Colonel Sutpen and his ambition to found a family; *The Unvanquished* (1938), a cycle of stories about the Sartoris dynasty; *The Wild Palms* (1939), half of which deals with a convict from back in the pine hills; *The Hamlet* (1940), a first novel about the Snopes clan, with others to follow; and *Go Down, Moses* (1942), in which Faulkner's principal theme is the relation between whites and Negroes. There are also many Yoknapatawpha stories in *These 13* (1931) and *Doctor Martino* (1934), besides other stories privately printed (like *Miss Zilphia Gant,* 1932) or published in magazines and still to be collected or used as episodes in novels.[1]

Just as Balzac, who may have inspired the series, divided his *Comédie Humaine* into "Scenes of Parisian Life," "Scenes of Provincial Life," "Scenes of Private Life," so Faulkner might divide his work into a number of cycles: one about the planters and their descendants, one about the townspeople of Jefferson, one about the poor whites, one about the Indians, and one about the Negroes. Or again, if he adopted a division by families, there would be the Compson-Sartoris saga, the continuing Snopes saga, the McCaslin saga, dealing with the white and black descendants of Carothers McCaslin, and the Ratliff-Bundren saga, devoted to the backwoods farmers of Frenchman's Bend. All the cycles or sagas are closely interconnected; it is as if each new book was a chord or segment of a total situation always existing in the author's mind. Some-

[1] That was the tally in 1945. With one exception, all the books that Faulkner published after that year are concerned with Yoknapatawpha County. The exception is *A Fable* (1954), about a reincarnated Christ in the First World War. The Yoknapatawpha books, eight in number, are *Intruder in the Dust* (1948), about a lynching that is averted by a seventy-year-old spinster and a pair of boys; *Knight's Gambit* (1949), recounting the adventures in detection of Gavin Stevens; *Collected Stories of William Faulkner* (1950), containing all the stories in *These 13* and *Doctor Martino* as well as several not previously collected; *Requiem for a Nun* (1951), a three-act drama, with narrative prologues to each act, about the later life of Temple Drake; *Big Woods* (1955), a cycle of hunting stories, some of them revised from chapters of *Go Down, Moses; The Town* (1957), second volume in the Snopes trilogy; *The Mansion* (1959), concluding the trilogy; and *The Reivers,* published a month before Faulkner's death on July 6, 1962. In all, sixteen of his books belong to the Yoknapatawpha cycle, as well as half of another book *(The Wild Palms)* and it is hard to count how many stories.

times a short story is the sequel to an earlier novel. For example, we read in *Sartoris* that Byron Snopes stole a packet of letters from Narcissa Benbow; and in "There Was a Queen," a story published five years later, we learn how Narcissa got the letters back again. Sometimes, on the other hand, a novel contains the sequel to a story; and we discover from an incidental reference in *The Sound and the Fury* that the Negro woman whose terror of death was portrayed in "That Evening Sun" had indeed been murdered and her body left in a ditch for the vultures. Sometimes an episode has a more complicated history. Thus, in the first chapter of *Sanctuary,* we hear about the Old Frenchman place, a ruined mansion near which the people of the neighborhood had been "digging with secret and sporadic optimism for gold which the builder was reputed to have buried somewhere about the place when Grant came through the country on his Vicksburg campaign." Later this digging for gold served as the subject of a story published in the *Saturday Evening Post:* "Lizards in Jamshyd's Courtyard." Still later the story was completely rewritten and became the last chapter of *The Hamlet.*[2]

As one book leads into another, the author sometimes falls into inconsistencies of detail. There is a sewing-machine agent named V. K. Suratt who appears in *Sartoris* and some of the stories written at about the same time. When we reach *The Hamlet,* his name has changed to Ratliff, although his character remains the same (and his age, too, for all the twenty years that separate the backgrounds of the two novels). Henry Armstid is a likable figure in *As I Lay Dying* and *Light in August;* in *The Hamlet* he is mean and half-demented. His wife, whose character remains consistent, is called Lula in one book and Martha in another; in the third she is nameless. There is an Indian chief named Doom who appears in several stories; he starts as the father of Issetibeha (in "Red Leaves") and ends as his nephew (in "A Justice"). The mansion called Sutpen's Hundred was built of brick at the beginning of *Absalom, Absalom!* but at the end of the novel it is all wood and inflammable except for the chimneys. But these errors are inconsequential, considering the scope of Faulkner's series; and I should judge that most of them are afterthoughts rather than oversights.

All his books in the Yoknapatawpha cycle are part of the same living pattern. It is this pattern, and not the printed volumes in which part of it is recorded, that is Faulkner's real achievement.

---

[2] The Old Frenchman place was built in the 1830s by Louis Grenier, as Faulkner tells us in the prologue to the first act of *Requiem for a Nun* (1951).

Its existence helps to explain one feature of his work: that each novel, each long or short story, seems to reveal more than it states explicitly and to have a subject bigger than itself. All the separate works are like blocks of marble from the same quarry: they show the veins and faults of the mother rock. Or else—to use a rather strained figure—they are like wooden planks that were cut, not from a log, but from a still living tree. The planks are planed and chiseled into their final shapes, but the tree itself heals over the wound and continues to grow. Faulkner is incapable of telling the same story twice without adding new details. In the present volume* I wanted to use part of *The Sound and the Fury,* the novel that deals with the fall of the Compson family. I thought that the last part of the book would be most effective as a separate episode, but still it depended too much on what had gone before. Faulkner offered to write a very brief introduction that would explain the relations of the characters. What he finally sent me is the much longer passage printed at the end of the volume: a genealogy of the Compsons from their first arrival in America. Whereas the novel is confined (except for memories) to a period of eighteen years ending on Easter Sunday, 1928, the genealogy goes back to the battle of Culloden in 1745, and forward to the year 1943, when Jason, last of the Compson males, has sold the family mansion, and Sister Caddy has last been heard of as the mistress of a German general. The novel that Faulkner wrote about the Compsons had long ago been given what seemed its final shape, but the pattern or body of legend behind the novel—and behind his other books— was still developing.

Although the pattern is presented in terms of a single Mississippi county, it can be extended to the Deep South as a whole; and Faulkner always seems conscious of its wider application. He might have been thinking of his own novels when he described the ledgers in the commissary of the McCaslin plantation, in *Go Down, Moses.* They recorded, he says, "that slow trickle of molasses and meal and meat, of shoes and straw hats and overalls, of plowlines and collars and heelbolts and clevises, which returned each fall as cotton"—in a sense they were local and limited; but they were also "the continuation of that record which two hundred years had not been enough to complete and another hundred would not be enough to discharge; that chronicle which was a whole land in miniature, which multiplied and compounded was the entire South."

*The Portable Faulkner [ed. note].

Cleanth Brooks

Faulkner the Provincial

Most readers associate William Faulkner with the South quite as automatically as they associate Thomas Hardy with Wessex, Robert Frost with northern New England, and William Butler Yeats with Ireland, and perhaps more naturally than they associate Dylan Thomas with Wales. The regions and cultures to which these writers are linked differ in character, but they all stand in sharp contrast to the culture of the great world cities of the twentieth century. They have in common a basically agricultural economy, a life of farms, villages, and small towns, an old-fashioned set of values, and a still vital religion with its cult, creed, and basic norms of conduct. Wessex is very different from Sligo; New Hampshire, from North Mississippi. But for all their differences, each provides its author with a vantage point from which to criticize, directly or perhaps merely by implication, the powerful metropolitan culture.

Thus Robert Frost has characteristically taken for his vantage point not the more populous, heavily urbanized southern half of New England but the gaunt, old-fashioned, and relatively poverty-stricken region of northern New England. It is a grave injustice to regard Frost as a local colorist, exploiting the attraction that the quaint and the folksy hold for a metropolitan audience. He can be, and has been, so misunderstood, but Frost is making a serious criticism of twentiety-century man, and his loving elaboration of the life of New Hampshire is no mere indulgence in picturesque sentimentality or the comedy of the American rustic.

From William Faulkner: The Yoknapatawpha Country *by Cleanth Brooks. Yale University Press, 1963. Copyright © by Yale University.*

So it is also with Yeats, whose Ireland stands over against London much as Faulkner's South stands over against New York. The parallels between the cultural situations of these two very different men are so interesting that they deserve detailed illustration. Like Yeats, Faulkner benefited immeasurably from the fact that his own country has shown a long cultural lag behind great commercial and intellectual centers like London and New York. Like Yeats again, Faulkner's sense of history and his sense of participation in a living tradition have been of the utmost importance. Faulkner's work, like that of the great Irish poet, embodies a criticism of the prevailing commercial and urban culture, a criticism made from the standpoint of a provincial and traditional culture.

An Irishman like Sean O'Faolain senses at once the similarity between the two provincial cultures (even though O'Faolain manages to misunderstand the use that Faulkner makes of his). From "what little I have seen of Mississippi," O'Faolain writes,

> and [from] all I have read about it, life there sounds very much like life in County Cork. There is the same passionate provincialism; the same local patriotism; the same southern nationalism—those long explicit speeches of Gavin Stevens in *Intruder in the Dust* might, *mutatis mutandis,* be uttered by a southern Irishman—the same feeling that whatever happens in Ballydehob or in Jefferson has never happened anywhere else before, and is more important than anything that happened in any period of history in any part of the cosmos; there is the same vanity of an old race; the same gnawing sense of old defeat; the same capacity for intense hatred; a good deal of the same harsh folk-humor; the same acidity; the same oscillation between unbounded self-confidence and total despair; the same escape through sport and drink.[1]

Such general likenesses are also discernible from this side of the Atlantic. Any Southerner who reads Yeats' *Autobiographies* is bound to be startled, over and over again, by the analogies between Yeats' "literary situation" and that of the Southern author: the strength to be gained from the writer's sense of belonging to a living community and the special focus upon the world bestowed by one's having a precise location in time and in history. But as the *Autobiographies* show, Yeats learned to distrust the sentimental patriot whose notions of literature worked through all the

[1] *The Vanishing Hero* (New York, Universal Library, 1957), p. 75.

obvious symbols—shamrocks, pepper pots made in the shape of
Irish round towers, harps, and books with green covers.[2] (In the
South, for shamrocks and round towers read magnolias and
Greek-revival porticoes.) Yeats learned too the fact that one's
worst literary enemies are sometimes to be found among one's
own people. He once consoled an English friend whose book of
poems had been soundly trounced in a Dublin newspaper by telling her that Dublin reviews were to be discounted; for years he
had instructed his London publishers not to send his books to the
Dublin papers for review. In London he could take his chance,
for the reviewer, if sometimes uncomprehending, had no special
cause to serve. But too often the Dublin journalist had to prove
his cosmopolitanism by giving the back of his hand to an Irish
book.[3] In the last fifty years Southern authors also have discovered
that their severest critics were to be found at home in the person
of reviewers who meant to show themselves just as emancipated
as the New York critics.

Through loyalty to his Irish provincialism—though it was
never a blind loyalty—Yeats converted potential weakness into a
position of strength. Faulkner has done something comparable,
making the provincial society out of which he comes, and with
which so much of his fiction deals, a positive resource—an instrument for developing and refining his meaning. But many readers
evidently regard Faulkner's provincial subject matter as a sheer
liability, or else they totally misconceive what he does with it.
After all, what can a provincial have to say of any consequence
to modern industrial man living in an age of electronics and nu-
clear power? Faulkner is preoccupied with the past and with a
rural setting, and what possible value can these have except perhaps as negative object lessons? Faulkner's treatment of history
is, then, a confirmation of our disowning the past, Faulkner's
famous county (obviously a rural slum) a way of reminding us how
far we have progressed.

If one trusts one's impression of the bulk of Faulkner criticism, these would seem to be typical ways in which Faulkner is
now being read. Much of it takes his fiction to be sociology—an
amateur and nonacademic sociology characterized by powerful
moral overtones. There is in such criticism a surreptitious com-
merce between sociological-historical fact and fictional meaning.
Particular insights and moral judgments that the critic has derived

[2] *Autobiographies* (New York, 1927), pp. 250–54.
[3] Allan Wade, ed., *The Letters of W. B. Yeats* (New York, 1955), p. 860.

from fictional contexts are smuggled across the frontier into the realm of historical fact and become generalizations about Southern culture. They are then cited as historical "fact" to prove the accuracy of the sweeping judgments of the Southern scene that are attributed to Faulkner.

Such shady methodological transactions are usually prompted by the highest motives. Whether they know it or not, most authors of Faulkner criticism are serious moralists, and they recognize that Faulkner is, in his own way, a moralist too. They want to take him seriously and this means that they are very much concerned with the factual substratum of Faulkner's mythical county.

In view of the situation, it might be wise to take a look at Faulkner's facts—at Faulkner as the sociologist of north Mississippi. For this purpose, one of the most useful articles I have ever encountered is that published a few years ago by Dr. Winthrop Tilley in the *American Journal of Mental Deficiency*.[4] In an article entitled "The Idiot Boy in Mississippi," he undertook to show that Benjy Compson of *The Sound and the Fury* is merely a "stuffed idiot," a "fabricated literary idiot," quite incredible on any literal level. Tilley maintains that on the basis of clinical evidence most idiots are "phlegmatic, indifferent, and comparatively unexcitable." Moreover, they are "low-geared sexually." Tilley finds it most unlikely that Faulkner's Benjy would ever have displayed toward the schoolgirls passing by his house the sexual interest which prompted his brother Jason to have him gelded.

Tilley finds that Faulkner is just as wide of the legal facts. He points out that there are cogent reasons for doubting that Benjy's gelding would ever have been permitted. He cites the Mississippi code which makes mayhem a penitentiary offence, and he adds a footnote pointing out that though Mississippi did in 1928 (fifteen years after Benjy's alleged gelding) legalize sterilization for "certain institutional individuals," "castration was specifically forbidden in the statute. Sec. 6957." Besides, Benjy would have had to be sent to the State School for the Feeble Minded at Ellisville, Mississippi, the state code (see Section 6907) specifically stipulating that "mere idiots" shall not be admitted to the institution at Jackson.

All of this is sufficiently devastating evidence of how little Faulkner's story of the life and times of Benjy Compson is to be taken as a sound medical and legal account of what can happen to idiots in Mississippi. Though the present case is extreme, any-

[4] *59* (1955), 374–77.

thing calculated to shake the reader's confidence in the literal accuracy of Faulkner's "facts" is probably to be commended. Faulkner's novels have too often been read not as fiction but as factual accounts, with the notion that they represent only slightly distorted pictures of Southern rural and small-town life.

But Dr. Tilley wrote his article not so much in defense of the good name of the state of Mississippi as in derogation of Faulkner's art, for he argues that Faulkner's failure to get his facts straight has seriously injured his novel. He can allow to *The Sound and the Fury* no higher praise than "interesting failure." The character of Benjy, he says, is too implausible to carry the fictional weight placed upon him.

This judgment is the more interesting in that most admirers of Faulkner would put *The Sound and the Fury* among his three or four finest novels, and many would account it—as apparently Faulkner himself did—his masterpiece. Moreover, many readers have felt Benjy to be quite convincing—including a colleague of mine who is a psychoanalyst. One does not know, he says, what really goes on in an idiot's mind, but Faulkner's dramatization of what goes on in Benjy's seems to him a plausible guess and in any case constitutes a convincing imaginative account.

What is of basic concern here is what is always of concern in literature: the relation of truth of fact to aesthetic value—of "truth of reference" to "truth of coherence." The relationship between the two truths is rarely a simple one. It is not a simple one in Faulkner's novels. Faulkner critics are prone to confuse matters by saying that since the fiction is good, the "facts" must be correct, or that since the facts are incorrect, the fiction is bound to be poor. Faulkner's novels and stories, properly read, can doubtless tell us a great deal about the South, but Faulkner is primarily an artist. His reader will have to respect the mode of fiction and not transgress its limitations if he is to understand from it the facts about the South—that is, he must be able to sense what is typical and what is exceptional, what is normal and what is an aberration. He can scarcely make these discriminations unless he is prepared to see what Faulkner is doing with his "facts."

This misplaced stress upon realism might seem to find its proper corrective in a compensating stress upon symbolism—not facts but what they point to, not Faulkner as sociologist but Faulkner as symbolist poet. Surely, such a general emphasis is sound, for no great literature is to be taken just literally, and even the simplest literature is symbolic in the sense that it is universal, representative, and finally exhibits Man, not merely individual men. But a good deal of Faulkner criticism has to be described as little better than symbol-mongering—and I mean by the term something morbid, excessive, and obsessed, a grotesque parody of anything like an adequate, careful reading. It magnifies details irresponsibly; it feverishly prospects for possible symbols and then forces them beyond the needs of the story. It views the novel not as a responsible context with its own network of interrelations but as a sort of grab bag out of which particular symbols can be drawn.

The symbol-mongers have been busy with Benjy, the idiot of *The Sound and the Fury.* Mrs. Compson, his mother, is a vain and superficial woman who feels it necessary to assert from time to time that her family is as good as that into which she has married. When it becomes plain that her child is condemned to idiocy, she insists upon changing his name from Maury to Benjy, since Maury is a name associated with her family, the Bascombs. Her motive is clear and, granted the nature of the woman, perfectly adequate. But one critic has seen in the name-changing evidence that the Compsons are really superstitious and primitive, since they evidently "assume that names have mysterious powers."[5] The Compson family's trouble, however, is not primitivism but decadence, not irrational belief but lack of belief. Mrs. Compson, for example, would be the better off for Dilsey's simple faith.

Again, because it would be "especially significant in the degradation of the Compsons,"[6] another commentator has discovered that Benjy—and the evidence is the flimsiest possible—has committed incest with Caddy, his sister. That this notion completely distorts Caddy's character and her whole relation to her afflicted brother apparently did not seem to be a matter of any importance. Faulkner is concerned to show the degradation of the Compsons, so to discover another bit of degradation—it does not matter what kind—is to help the author along.[7] The "fact" (of incest) has been manufactured out of "symbolic" appropriateness.

Anthropology has been used on occasion to throw startling

[5] Barbara M. Crossman, *"The Sound and the Fury:* The Pattern of Sacrifice," *Arizona Quarterly, 16* (1960), 11.

[6] George R. Stewart and Joseph M. Backus, "'Each in Its Ordered Place': Structure and Narration in Benjy's Section of *The Sound and the Fury," American Literature, 29* (1958), 455n. Carvel Collins has disposed of this notion in his "Miss Quentin's Paternity Again," *Texas Studies in Language and Literature, 2* (1960), 253–60.

[7] Mr. Backus writes that "if Faulkner sought to picture Southern decadence, an incestuous affair between his heroine and her idiot brother provides the finishing touch." See his "Names and Characters in Faulkner's *The Sound and the Fury," Names, 6* (1958), 228–29.

light upon the Compson family. In *The Golden Bough* we are told that in Burma adulterers kill a pig to atone for their crime and pray that the hills and streams will be healed. Now someone has noted that the Compsons kill a pig for their Christmas dinner, but that they do it without penitence and without expressing any wish for atonement.[8] This is so ingenious that the voice of common sense may seem that of a churlish spoilsport. Yet only one of the Compsons, Uncle Maury, is an adulterer, and Uncle Maury is not a Burmese. Shall there be no more innocent consumption of pork chops and spareribs in Yoknapatawpha County because someone has read *The Golden Bough?*

When Quentin, in his agony over Caddy's having given herself to her lover, proposes killing her and then killing himself, he takes out a knife and holds it to her throat. One critic suggests that Quentin "symbolically" wants to perform a hysterectomy—that is, to remove "the agent [sic] of Caddy's (and the family's) sin."[9] But there is something far-fetched about trying to make Quentin even symbolically a Jack the Ripper, and the suggestion is not rendered any more plausible by the portion of Caddy's anatomy at which Quentin points his knife.

Quentin's section of *The Sound and the Fury* is dated June 2. It has been proposed that perhaps he did not actually drown himself until after midnight, in which case his death would have occurred at an especially appropriate time, for June 3 is the birthday of Jefferson Davis, the president of the Confederacy.[10] The notion would seem to be that Quentin's downfall is somehow tied to the downfall of the Old South. But there is no hint in the novel that Quentin knew that it was the eve of Jefferson Davis' birthday or that he meant to postpone his death until 1:00 A.M. Eastern Standard Time. Faulkner could have saved Quentin the wait by simply assigning his section to June 3 in the first place.

These instances of symbol-hunting are extreme, but they are only a little less absurd than much respectable commentary on Faulkner. Any useful criticism must do more than provide an aimless and mechanical notation of symbols. It must make its account of symbolic events and scenes coherent and responsible by relating the alleged symbols to the total fictional context.

It might be supposed that sociologizing and symbol-mongering are antithetical faults, but they can, and do, occur side by side. Indeed, both aberrations have to be regarded as different

[8] Crossman, pp. 12–13.

[9] Earle Labor, in *Explicator, 17* (1959), Item 29.

[10] Stewart and Backus, *American Literature, 29,* 453, n. 10.

ways of evading the central critical task: to determine and evaluate the meaning of the work in the fullness of its depth and amplitude. The excessive literalism which converts the fictional into factual events and thus yields "sociology" is a counterpart of the misguided yearning for universal meanings which produces the perversities of symbol-mongering.

Some knowledge of how life is actually lived (and has been lived) in Mississippi would have prevented the writing of much nonsense. An awareness of how fiction "works" would have helped even more. Faulkner, to be sure, has much to tell us about life in Mississippi and in the South generally. He is indeed concerned with human beings and human values. But his novels are neither case studies nor moral treatises. They are works of art and have to be read as such.

Olga W. Vickery

The Figure in the Carpet

With *The Reivers* Yoknapatawpha County, consisting of
some 2400 square miles and inhabited, according to William
Faulkner's private census, by a population of 15,611 has received
its last topographical, historical, and legendary delineation.
Accordingly, Faulkner's works, so often placed in the tradition of
the fictional saga, can now be set over against and distinguished
from the achievements of Balzac, Zola, and Galsworthy as well
as of his own contemporaries such as C. P. Snow or Anthony
Powell.

The chief interest in linking him to this tradition is not to see
what he has assimilated or copied but what he has achieved that
is uniquely his own. And this involves identifying what Henry
James called "The Figure in the Carpet," "the thing that most
makes [the writer] apply himself, the thing without the effort to
achieve which he wouldn't write at all, the very passion of his
passion, the part of the business in which, for him, the flame of
art burns most intensely." Certainly Faulkner's uniqueness is not
to be found in a chronological rendering of events and characters
such as Malcolm Cowley suggests in his introduction to *The
Portable Faulkner.* Nor is it revealed in the essentially topographical arrangement of material in the *Collected Stories of William
Faulkner.* Such patterns, whatever their intrinsic value, fail to
penetrate to the heart of his work if only because they ignore the
formal strategies invoked by Faulkner. Similarly, the attempts,
beginning with George Marion O'Donnell, to focus on Faulkner's

From The Novels of William Faulkner: A Critical Interpretation *by Olga
W. Vickery. Louisiana State University Press, rev. ed., 1964. Copyright
© by Louisiana State University Press.*

morality, social criticism, or philosophy fall short of the mark. There is, of course, no doubt that ideas, moral judgment, and social criticism do exist or can be derived from his work. Yet they too are part of the texture of the carpet as Faulkner himself implies when he states quite categorically that the character is more important than the idea and that "the writer is not really interested in bettering man's condition. . . . He's interested in all man's behavior with no judgment whatever." (267)[1] In other words, moral and social dimensions emanate from the character and not vice versa.

Even the most casual of glances shows us that Faulkner's ability to "create flesh-and-blood people that will stand up and cast a shadow" (47) is a prominent part of the figure in the carpet. The sense of the density and complexity of life, the tremendous range and variety of character in his works has not been equalled in American literature. The Sartorises, the Snopeses, the Compsons, and the McCaslins; young Temple Drake sowing her wild oats (if such a metaphor can be disengaged from the male sex) in a house of prostitution; Lena Grove serenely licking sardine oil from her fingers; Ike Snopes ambling after his beloved cow through the long, golden afternoon; Dilsey, Nancy Mannigoe, Ringo, T. P.—the list seems endless at least partly because even minor characters, merely rounding out a scene or two, clamor for the reader's attention and understanding.

That they do so is a result of Faulkner's concern with the possibilities—including self-contradiction—inherent in character. As he has stated: "Those characters to me are quite real and quite constant. They are in my mind all the time. I don't have any trouble at all going back to pick up one. I forget what they did, but the character I don't forget, and when the book is finished, that character is not done, he still is going on at some new devilment that sooner or later I will find out about and write about." (78) In addition to this independence and ingenuity, these characters also have the delightful ability to create their own milieu by dragging in a number of people whom Faulkner claims he had never anticipated, never seen nor heard before. For example, Byron Snopes in *Sartoris,* writing lewd letters to Narcissa Benbow and absconding with the bank's cash, has called forth a whole swarm of Snopeses, including a senator, a murderer, and an idiot, as well as his own spawn—a foursome precociously ingenious in

---

[1] All quotations of Faulkner's personal opinions are from F. L. Gwynn and J. L. Blotner (eds.), *Faulkner in the University* (Charlottesville, Va., 1959).

their viciousness, eating pedigreed dogs and busily attempting to
burn one of their kinsmen at the stake.

Clearly, then, Faulkner's major concern is not with manipulat-
ing his characters nor with documenting the stages in their development. Instead, having granted them their autonomy and
having assumed that all men are capable of all things, he has concentrated on exploring and revealing their complexity. For instance, one thinks of Boon Hogganbeck first as the camp buffoon,
the hunter incapable of hitting a barn door at twenty paces or the
petulant child intent on protecting his tree full of squirrels from
other hunters. Yet he is also the man who has enough courage
and patience to tame Lion and enough love to avenge his in-
juries by killing Old Ben with only his knife for a weapon. Demanding a rarer courage as well as compassion and understanding
is his willingness to help Sam Fathers fulfill his wish not to outlive
Lion and Old Ben—a willingness that Shakespeare's Antony
could not command in his faithful servant, Eros. In *The Reivers*
Boon's marksmanship is once more presented in highly comic
terms, but beyond that he achieves his final definition, surprisingly enough, as Yoknapatawpha's Don Quixote finding his Dul-
cinea in Everbe Corinthia, one of Miss Reba's girls, but without
the good knight's subsequent disenchantment. For in the world of
The Reivers, the real and the ideal can be reconciled and so lead
to the fairy-tale conclusion—the marriage of Boon and Everbe.

Boon is, of course, representative of many of Faulkner's characters who disconcert critics looking for consistency and the logic
of cause and effect. But Faulkner's indifference to such formal
patterns of history frees him to recognize an integral, experiential
unity which can encompass both change and apparent contradiction: "To me they are people, and they have grown older as I
have grown older, and probably they have changed a little—my
concept of them has changed a little, as they themselves have
changed and I changed. That they have grown. I know more
about people than I knew when I first thought of them, and they
have become more definite to me as people." (108) Accordingly,
he as well as the reader may discover a latent characteristic that
manifests itself only under the pressure of some new stimulus or
situation. For example, there is development but no inconsistency
in Gavin Stevens from *Light in August* to *Requiem for a Nun.*
But in *The Town* under the impact of Eula, herself transformed
by virtue of her devotion to her child and De Spain, he discovers
a hitherto unsuspected capacity for dreaming and for suffering
the agony of frustration and failure.

Perhaps a more characteristic way of exploring the latent possibilities of character is Faulkner's repeated use of juxtaposed scenes involving either a lapse of time or a change of place, leading the reader to recognize both simultaneity and progression. Caddy, the child, getting her panties dirty or observing Nancy Mannigoe's mounting panic and despair in "That Evening Sun" coexists with "the ageless and beautiful, cold serene and damned mistress of a German staff general" described in the appendix to the Modern Library edition of *The Sound and the Fury.* (12) And Nancy herself is at once the fearful wife whose infidelities have been discovered, the raucous voice that refuses to be stilled as it demands payment for services rendered to the Baptist deacon, the murderer of Temple Drake's child, and the embodiment of faith asking Temple only to "Believe."

Equally effective is Faulkner's technique of a fallible narrator or point-of-view figure who recognizes and attempts to correct his own mistakes in perception or his own limitations of understanding as the narrator does in "Hair," or the use of multiple narrators who contradict, correct, supplement, and even invent as they do in the Snopes trilogy. And finally, rhetoric itself can serve to modulate or transform the reader's view of a character. In "The Long Summer" the animal-like viciousness of Mink Snopes (suggested by his very name) is linked to his obsessive determination to revenge himself first on Houston and then on Flem. In *The Mansion* the comic horror of these scenes modulates into the vision, still comic but replacing horror with pathos, of his abortive escape from Parchman prison, wearing a woman's dress and bonnet, to the unmodified pathos of his release. The smallness of his figure and his almost total ignorance of the world into which he has finally been released introduce a child-like quality into his composite portrait, a child who must perform the act he has set himself though he has long ago forgotten his own reasons for so doing.

Yet if the limitless possibility of character is a striking and significant part of the Faulknerian carpet, an equally important aspect is Faulkner's concern with the personal identity and common humanity of his characters. The fascination exerted by the problem of identify is nowhere more graphically rendered than in those conscious, deliberate exercises in self-definition embarked upon by so many of Faulkner's characters. Here we see another facet of the author's concern with human possibilities, for not only does he probe for the uniqueness, the quiddity of individuals, but he also charts the variety of ways in which the knowledge of identity both is and is not acquired. Chick Mallison, Isaac McCaslin, Lucas Beauchamp, Joe Christmas, and Charles Etienne Bon, each in his own way exhibits the successes, the hazards, and the failures involved in human identity. But in each case identity is contingent upon a precise relationship to the common humanity of mankind. For Faulkner, common humanity seems to resolve itself into the capacity to aspire and so to choose acceptance, rejection, or evasion of the eternal verities—courage, honor, pride, compassion, pity. Because of his freedom to choose and because his identity is the sum of his choices, the individual character is both intricately woven into the warp and woof of Faulkner's carpet and rendered in a variety of poses and actions that reflect their author's quizzical delight and curiosity at the products of their freedom: "the writer is learning all the time he writes and he learns from his own people, once he has conceived them truthfully and has stuck to the verities of human conduct, human behavior, human aspiration, then he learns—yes, they teach him, they surprise him, they teach him things that he didn't know. . . ." (96)

If Faulkner is indeed concerned not only to explore the range of possibility in character but to probe for its essential humanity, no matter how shrivelled, he must have complete freedom to proceed in any order, in any temporal or spatial direction, and to recall and reexamine any action, situation, or character from a new perspective. Consequently, he experiments endlessly not because, like Henry James, he is interested in form and technique as values in themselves but because no single method can accomplish his purpose of rendering the unique figure of his carpet. The difference between the two is clear. James is the most conscious and consummately skillful craftsman America has ever produced; Faulkner is the most dedicated student of human nature, driven by the demon of compassionate curiosity to literary experimentation.

It follows, then, that Faulkner's interest in form and technique cannot be divorced from his interest in character, his determination, as in *Absalom, Absalom!* or *Light in August,* to make the reader aware simultaneously of consistency and contradiction, immersion in and transcendence of time, simplicity as well as complexity, depth as well as scope. To do this he resists any temptation to circumscribe, define, or interpret his characters from a position of authority since that would immediately destroy their autonomy. Thus, he goes a step beyond the Joycean artist who refines himself out of existence. In Faulkner, authorial exclusion is replaced by authorial transcendence. The anonymous Voice so often detected in his fiction is the author seeing himself distanced as one more perspective on the scene, one more legitimate but not conclusive point of view. It is also his mature version of the omniscient narrator founded upon the conviction that freedom for the self is freedom from the self. Throughout, his aim is to avoid limiting the freedom of character, reader, or author.

An apparent contradiction, often pointed out by critics, actually serves to reinforce these statements. Popeye, the cardboard figure, the two-dimensional character, the mechanical man, seems completely circumscribed, an impression that is supported by the awkwardly introduced "case history" summarizing his heredity and environment. But this Zolaesque tendency to "explain" is held in check by Faulkner's own and apparently instinctive desire to provoke simple curiosity. The sociological-psychological mold is broken as Popeye passively accepts death for a crime he can prove he has not committed and by his final words to his executioner "Fix my hair, Jack." The inhuman monster conditioned to callousness shows a fleeting trace of wry irony if not humor as he repudiates that minimal life so precariously and persistently maintained at the expense of living.

Faulkner's proper concern, then, is to preserve the heart of the mystery by ordering his material to provide a maximum of concentration, illumination, and implication. In other words, Faulkner, the self-styled "failed poet," (22) makes prose fiction approximate poetry which he equates with the lyric and defines as "some moving, passionate moment of the human condition distilled to its absolute essence." (202) Such an attempt does not simply demand absolute exactitude; it also encourages the soaring design of rhetoric, the evocative condensation of imagery and symbolism, and the variety of textural richness as well as dramatic immediacy, all characteristic of Faulkner's style at its best.

In viewing the carpet one therefore moves inevitably from an awareness of vibrantly living characters to the perception of an intricately related series of lyrical stases. Individually these recall Keats's Grecian Urn capturing the essence of the moment, while collectively they constitute a modern prose equivalent to the Renaissance lyric cycle such as the *Amoretti*. It is with this that the place and significance of Faulkner's short stories in his total canon begin to emerge. In terms of content, we distinguish between stories, like "Turnabout," that are completely outside the Yoknapatawpha saga and those that contribute to it. The former serve as a variegated peripheral frieze that frames the panorama of the central saga. At the same time, the thematic and narrative similarities between a story like "Honor" and a novel like *Pylon,* both concerned with a bizarre solution to a sexual triangle, suggest the possibility of alternative or additional sagas that were never developed.

It is, however, the Yoknapatawpha stories that show the three-fold function of the short story in Faulkner: as a narrative unit in its own right, as an element of structure, and as a method of thematic and character exploration. These stories may be classified roughly as adjunctive, projective, and parodic. The first, the adjunctive, are stories that simply add more information about certain characters, situations. or the history of Yoknapatawpha County: for example, the MacCallums in "The Tall Men," the Griers in "Two Soldiers" and "Shall Not Perish," or Miss Emily in "A Rose for Emily" and Miss Minnie Cooper in "Dry September." Others, such as "There Was a Queen" or "All the Dead Pilots," examine a new aspect of characters already established and so project new demands of action on the characters and new demands of understanding on the readers. Thus, the laughing face of Johnny Sartoris is replaced by an inarticulate, humorless man incapable of seeing the comic aspects of his rivalry with a superior officer for the favors of a girl so eager to accommodate all men that she is nicknamed "Kitchener." The final group, consisting mainly of the Indian stories, parody the white man's follies and ways so as to counterpoint the design of the primary saga itself. A pair of useless red shoes serves as a symbol of status and authority, the wilderness and the vanished past form a subject of nostalgic reminiscence; while the "Negro question," that is, the question of his position in the Indian economy, is the subject of a hilarious debate about whether cannibalism offers a sensible solution to Negro fecundity. But most impressive as illumination through parody is the ritual pursuit of a Negro slave in "Red Leaves." The desperate terror, the agony, the pain of his gangrenous arm leap out of the scene with a dramatic immediacy that both points up and is underscored by the essentially comic view of his pursuers moving in their decorous, stately, untroubled course.

In addition to the pattern of content there is a pattern of form and structure. Its first aspect consists of a group of conventional stories depending on plot complication and action leading to some sort of resolution, as in "Dr. Martino," "The Brooch," or "Artist at Home." Since most of these stories are unrelated to the Yoknapatawpha saga and its techniques of presentation, they can fairly be viewed as providing a bold relief background for the scenes, actions, and characters that dominate the center of the carpet. A second group approximates the lyric insofar as it tends to focus on a single effect and a single impression. The emphasis is on situations rather than plot and on revelation rather than definition of character. Typical of these are "A Rose for Emily" and "That Evening Sun," surely two of Faulkner's finest stories. In the latter the situation is so vividly rendered and Nancy's fears so powerfully communicated that her death has, at times, been taken for granted and her corpse identified with the bones picked clean by buzzards in *The Sound and the Fury.* But in view of her disconcerting resurrection in *Requiem for a Nun,* a careful re-reading discovers how much emphasis is placed upon the foolishness of her fears. As in "That Evening Sun" so in "Dry September" or "Wash," Faulkner's refusal to dramatize the conclusive action serves both to intensify the dominant emotion and to project it beyond the story itself. By this last Faulkner makes the reader implicitly accept the possibility of future continuation of the narrative and recognize that his characters' lives extend beyond the formal confines of individual works. Questions remain unanswered as to the fate of young Sartoris Snopes fleeing from his barn-burning father, Dewey Dell still carrying her child as the Bundren family begins its homeward journey, or Byron Bunch whose inept but earnest advances are firmly repelled by Lena Grove.

With the third type of story, a new element in the design of Faulkner's carpet can now be detected. In addition to living characters and frozen moments of concentrated emotion, the carpet also contains a series of recurring designs. For, surprisingly enough in view of his concern with freedom, the third kind of story is formulaic. Faulkner describes its genesis and function to a University of Virginia student: "There are so few plots and what you read—the plot has not changed too much, only the people involved in it have changed, and to see the same plot repeated time after time with different people motivated by it or trying to cope with it, you can learn about people that way, to match your own experience with living people." (117) What would seem to reveal a paucity of imagination becomes in his hands a highly sophisticated technique, a most subtle method of exploring character and delineating its uniqueness. The formula, which Faulkner calls "the dead skeleton," is born of curiosity meeting the challenge to human freedom and imaginatively evoking characters whose vibrancy animates and fleshes out the dead skeleton resident in the human situation.

The skeleton or formula consists of two main patterns or types, each of which possesses three sub-types or variants. And since each is capable of interrelation, there are at least nine possible formulaic modes. The first main pattern is that of the contest, whether involving cards, horses, or women. If emphasis is placed on the formal aspect of the contest—the complicated moves and countermoves of a card game, the intricate maneuvers of bargaining, the wild ingenuity of sexual rivals—and if the opponents are evenly matched, the result is likely to be comic. *The Reivers* offers the purest form of comedy, for in the inherently absurd process of exchanging a car for a horse in order to regain the car, nobody wins and nobody loses. Similarly, Ab Snopes, before he becomes soured, and Pat Stamper are, in the story "Flem," so evenly matched in ingenuity and so obviously enjoying their contest that the elaborate swapping of horses and mules and even milk separators is hilariously funny.

In contrast, Miss Rosa's ability in "Raid" to dupe the Yankees into providing her with a steady stream of mules fuses the comic with the heroic. The increasing stakes in "Was" ultimately involving the fate of a confirmed bachelor, a frustrated spinster, and two Negro slaves introduce an element of irony. Of greater mordancy is the game of checkers in "The Long Summer" between Mink and Lump Snopes, played in an atmosphere of macabre humor and nightmare pressure. It is, however, "Spotted Horses," the most famous of Faulkner's horse-trade stories, pitting amateurs against professionals and introducing the themes of greed and exploitation, that offers the widest range of tones. The absurdity of the situation, the irrational behavior of the participants, and the exaggerated humor of incident is qualified by the pathetic suffering of Mrs. Armstid, the horrifying transformation of her husband, and the accidental involvement of Tull and his family. Thus, the simple formula is made to yield a complex insight into human behavior, morality, responsibility, and justice.

The final version of the contest formula involves some form of sexual rivalry. The Queen Bee—the irresistible, elusive She—as exemplified by Mink Snopes's wife making a private harem out of her father's lumber camp is broadly comic. As Eula Varner unleashes a frenzy of desire and frustration in the young men of Frenchman's Bend, comedy is fused with myth and symbol, but as Temple Drake alternates between provocation and retreat, the dominant tone is horror. The classic triangle, like the mass pursuit, appears in many guises. In "A Courtship" Herman Basket's sister marries her uncompetitive suitor while the other two are busily engaged in eating and racing contests. When the triangle involves adultery, the range of response becomes more complex. In "Centaur in Brass" Tom Tom farcically chases Turl, his wife's lover, until both fall breathlessly into a ditch and reestablish their friendship and male solidarity. In "Wild Palms," however, the attempt of Charlotte's husband to help the man who has not only run away with but also inadvertently killed his wife is developed not as knock-about comedy but as shrill, highly-colored melodrama. And beyond it the basic triangle reappears in *Pylon* as the continuing *ménage a trois* in which not even Laverne knows who has fathered her child. Here melodramatic situation is used to develop with the artless simplicity of a morality play the theme of paternity as an emotional and moral rather than legal commitment. When adultery is set in a racial context, the formula develops added ramifications including those of ambiguity and uncertainty. Thus Lucas Beauchamp regains his wife from Zack Carothers in "The Fire and the Hearth" and simultaneously recognizes that his victory may be transitory; indeed, his very suspicion may be groundless. And at the furthest extreme from the comic there is the unrelieved horror of incest compounded by miscegenation in "The Bear" as Ike relives the scene of old Carothers McCaslin calling his Negro daughter to his bed.

The other main pattern used by Faulkner is the hunt in which the prime objects are buried treasure, wild game, or human beings. Thus, as engaged in by Lucas Beauchamp, the search for buried treasure provides a wide spectrum of humor. But a similar hunt contrived by Flem Snopes results in a shattering experience for the Armstid family and a chastening one for Ratliff. Accordingly, both the victim and the victimizer evoke a horror which replaces the original comic response.

In contrast the ritual pursuit of game is almost always treated seriously, though the mode may vary from heroic to elegiac to low mimetic. The heroic culminates in the poetic rhetoric of "The Bear" where through Sam Fathers, Isaac McCaslin, Old Ben and Lion, the story acquires a symbolic universality, testing not only courage but humility and integrity. In an elegiac mood, the aged Isaac in "Delta Autumn" watches the wilderness receding, the hunters refusing to discriminate between worthy game and does and fawns. On the periphery are such stories as "A Bear Hunt" that degenerates into a private joke or "A Fox Hunt" in which a cuckolded husband relieves his jealousy and mounting frustration by chasing a fox and finally killing it in a particularly brutal fashion.

The final object of the chase, that of another human being, may be pursued with two different aims. The hunt can either issue in death, as with lynching or scapegoat tales, or in life, as with the Reluctant Lover stories. And in either case they too range from comedy to tragedy. The vigorous chase of Tomey's Turl by Uncle Buck and Uncle Buddy, parodying the lynch tale, is comic because there is no possibility of violence or death. Comedy through parody is also used in "Red Leaves." Unhurried, patient, and meticulous about the rules to be followed, the Negro's Indian pursuers prefer to wait for their quarry to surrender rather than to track him down. But in "Dry September" and "Pantaloon in Black" as well as in *Light in August* and *Intruder in the Dust,* humor is either entirely absent or reduced to a caustic irony, for here there is no parody, only naked inhumanity to man.

When the human being is pursued as a sexual object, the stories offer brilliant variations on the theme of the Obsessed and the Reluctant Lover. The former, as in "Eula," frequently plays a complimentary role to the Queen Bee. But he is also seen in Philip St. Just Backhouse ("My Grandmother Millard") overcoming Melisandre's modesty, Hawkshaw ("Hair") patiently waiting for his Susan Reed to grow up, or Ike ("The Long Summer") happily following his beloved cow. When the Obsessed Lover is a woman, humor is replaced by an intensity bordering on hysteria whether it involves Miss Emily's ("A Rose for Emily") bizarre manner of claiming Homer Baron for her own, Miss Elly's determination ("Miss Elly") to kill herself and the recalcitrant Paul Montigny, or Joanna Burden pursuing Joe Christmas through her garden. The Obsessed Lover may also find that his obsession does not prevent him from feeling reluctant to satisfy it because of fear of involvement, difficulty of removing ingrained conviction, or loss of dignity, detachment, and simple male freedom. The strategies of evasion may encompass Houston's departure from Jefferson, Labove's attempted rape which will permit him to be forceful instead of humbly tentative, or the Reporter's conviction that he can become part of Laverne's world without sexual involvement. Depending on his character, then, we may feel a greater or lesser degree of sympathy for the lover, but we are rarely, if ever, free of a sense of the absurdity with which his obsession and his evasions surround him.

Broadly speaking, these formula stories, whether separate units or episodes within novels, contribute three major qualities: revelation of character, as in "Dry September," "Death Drag," or "The Bear"; recurrence of patterns, as in "Centaur in Brass,"

"A Courtship," and Artist at Home," each of which issues in a reconciliation of husband and lover; and diversity of tones as exhibited in "Was," "Pantaloon in Black," "Dry September" or in the love stories beginning with the romantic comedy of Melisandre and Lieutenant Philip St. Just Backhouse in "My Grandmother Millard" and its parody in the homosexual relationship of "A Divorce in Naples" and in Ike's attachment to the cow. The first of these qualities reiterates in a graphic, sketch-like fashion the centrality of character and personal identity. The second, the perception of the recurrence of a relatively limited number of patterns of human action, introduces into the Faulknerian design the perdurable limiting conditions of human existence. We become aware of our common humanity through perceiving the anatomical similarities of skeletons. Or, to put it otherwise, because in one sense there are so few courses of human action and they are pursued so repetitively, we see both the limitations of life and its ritualistic significance as the embodier of the eternal verities. If this awareness of recurring patterns suggests a straitening of human freedom and variety in the Faulknerian design, it is more than offset by the third quality, that of the brilliant diversity of tones exhibited in and through the formulas. By varying his tone and attitude from comedy through irony, heroism, pathos, and elegy to tragedy, Faulkner reveals in a deeper light the true nature of human freedom. It consists not so much in limitless opportunities for all conceivable actions as in an infinite variety of responses to those actions which man either can or must perform. In short, the diversity of tones constitutes that virtually unparalleled range of shading and color which amazes and delights every viewer of Faulkner's carpet.

This somewhat lengthy discussion of the types of short story simplifies our consideration of the novels since the short story for Faulkner is not only a genre but an element of structure. For Faulkner would accept Poe's statement that "unless a book follows a simple direct line such as a story of adventure, it becomes a series of pieces." The author's function, then, is to exercise "his judgment and taste to arrange the different pieces in the most effective place in juxtaposition to one another." (45) It is therefore possible to argue, as Malcolm Cowley does, that all of Faulkner's novels reveal some structural weakness, some absence of unity, and that he has no talent for sustained narrative and hence his reputation will eventually rest on his superbly structured short stories.

But it is also possible to assert that such criticism is irrelevant in that it uses the criteria of the well-made novel in discussing a form which deliberately rejects that particular tradition. In other words, Faulkner was creating a new form which would suit his own purpose: "You write a story to tell about people, man in his constant struggle with his own heart, with the hearts of others, or with his environment. It's man in the ageless, eternal struggle which we inherit and we go through as though they'd never happened before, shown for a moment in a dramatic instant of the furious motion of being alive, that's all any story is. You catch this fluidity which is human life and you focus a light on it and you stop it long enough for people to be able to see it." (239)

Clearly the light focussed and held is one of the structural principles underlying the form Faulkner evolved. In virtually all his works there are scenes which dramatically render a character's individuality so powerfully and unforgettably that they are climactic moments regardless of where they occur in the narrative. It is this principle which Faulkner developed out of the short story with its emphasis on the single incident and the character scrupulously revealed in a specific but universal moment of history. At the same time, he recognized that fiction could not truly exist as merely dramatic scenes involving individual human beings: "I mean that love and money and death are the skeletons on which the story is laid. They have nothing to do with the aspirations and conflicts of the human hearts involved. But the story has got to have some skeleton, and the skeletons are love or money or death." (198) The skeleton, then, is Faulkner's other structural principle, the one which provides the varieties of narrative development out of which emerge the recurrent themes and the characters' link with "man in the ageless, eternal struggles." When the two principles are mastered, Faulkner begins to bring his new form to fruition. Their presence and the result appear most obviously in his story-novels: *The Unvanquished, The Hamlet, Go Down, Moses,* and *Knight's Gambit.* To see them as ordered by the concepts of universal pattern and unique character is to grasp the true relationship of their parts and to avoid seeing nothing but what Cowley has called "a series of beads on a string."

Closely related to the story-novel is the novel of formal juxtaposition as seen in *The Sound and the Fury* and *As I Lay Dying.* But instead of focussing on a significant action, the emphasis is on a single, fixed attitude or state of mind, revealing itself through interior monologues as it responds to certain focal experiences in the past as well as to the demanding present. Each member of the Bundren family, for example, reacts in his own individual manner to Addie's death and to the crises of the funeral journey, just as each of the Compson brothers copes with the present while he reveals himself as in some sense molded by his past response to Caddy and her loss of virginity. The brilliant juxtaposition of psychological perspectives enables Faulkner to introduce and reinforce certain obvious comparisons and contrasts, to provide an infinite number of variations, and to achieve an incredible richness of texture and shading. To use but one example, Jason Compson's compusive greed for money is juxtaposed against Quentin's guilt about the financial sacrifice involved in his attending Harvard, Benjy's loss of the pasture—one of the three things he loved —Dilsey's indifference about whether or not Jason pays her, and Luster's anxious search for the lost quarter which will enable him to attend a travelling show.

When we turn to the counterpoint novels such as *The Wild Palms, Requiem for a Nun,* and *Light in August* (which, however, bears certain resemblances to the next type), the separateness of the stories is deliberately stressed. The very absence of narrative bridges creates that sustained comparison and contrast which leads to recognition of the uniqueness of character. It also bears in upon us in tentative, hypothetical fashion the possible metaphysical significance of the pattern in the carpet through recurring but sudden glimpses of the relation of identity and diversity, of the particular and the universal. Whether we call it point and counterpoint or theme and variation, the balancing of disparate stories is necessary in order to prevent a definitive, completed statement of theme or a single, sustained tone, which, in effect, would limit or predetermine the reader's response.

Thus, in *The Wild Palms* the romantic love of Henry and Charlotte results in a mismanaged abortion, her death, and his imprisonment. The emotional impact of their love is balanced by the Tall Convict, the ultimate version of the Reluctant Lover, forced into responsibility for a pregnant woman whom he neither knows, loves, nor desires. Tragedy and comedy; abortion and death as well as birth and life; prison as punishment and prison as reward: the evocative parallels can, of course, be multiplied. And yet they are without point unless the material's diversity is also fully recognized. Alternation between opposing character attitudes (as in *The Wild Palms*), differing authorial points of view (as in *Requiem for a Nun*), or disparate concepts (as in *Light in August*), all point up striking variations in surface configurations and disparate, multi-levelled clashing planes much after the manner of a Cézanne or cubist painting. The aim is simultaneously a perception of hitherto unnoticed similarities and a renewed awareness of the incontrovertible differences that exist both in the physical and in the more broadly human worlds.

Unlike the other counterpoint novels, *Light in August* does connect its three stories through plot, though only tangentially. But the real richness and coherence in this novel is due to the recurrence of the scapegoat pattern with its evocation of mythology and religion as it is enacted by Gail Hightower, Joanna Burden, and Joe Christmas. In the same way, the angular contrasts of diversity, providing a wide spectrum between the poles of life and death, are seen in the varied sexual relationships as well as in their conceptual clash with the religious modes of the novel.

The final distinguishable form, one that is among Faulkner's most original and certainly most misunderstood is what (for lack of a better word) I have called the "fused novel" which combines the virtues of the short story possessing its own "unity and coherence, the proper emphasis and integration which a long chronicle doesn't have" (108) with the illusion of density and complexity of life typical of the novel proper. This form may attempt to incorporate already existent stories or to make the illumination but embryonic or potential story an integral part of the novel. As a separate story, for example, "Barn Burning" emphasizes the vengefulness of Ab Snopes and the agony of the child, Sartoris Snopes, who can neither approve of nor betray his father. When it recurs in *The Hamlet,* it is narrated by Ratliff with his usual sardonic humor. The boy is not mentioned and the viciousness of Ab is transferred to Mink. What remains is a comic story which stresses the mounting frustration of De Spain, the imperturbability of Ab, and an indirect warning to Will Varner, his son Jody, and Frenchman's Bend. In addition, it is precisely because Jody hears this story that he begins that process of placating Flem that leads to his own dispossession. The integration of the story into a large unit is thus completed.

The use of the embryonic or potential short story is most clearly seen in *Absalom, Absalom!* Quentin and Shreve provide the novel's formal unity by virtue of their concern to explore the past as seen in the history of the Sutpen family. But there are at least three different accounts of Sutpen which could stand independently. In addition, because Quentin and Shreve are attempting an aesthetic reconstruction, they tend to think in terms of scenes and episodes: Miss Rosa's reaction to Sutpen's brutal proposal, Charles Etienne's tragic inability to define himself racially, Wash

Jones and his daughter Milly, Sutpen's adventures in Haiti, Charles Bon's doomed relationship with his mistress. Yet one is not conscious of the separateness of these stories because they are caught up in the fluidity of time and because they are an integral part of the total pattern of the book.

These unremitting efforts at formal experimentation testify to Faulkner's passionate effort to enshrine in his carpet the full quiddity of the living character, the lyrical exaltation of the moment that epitomizes, the sobering (even when most humorous) recognition of the unsought recurrence of human actions, and the emancipatory release afforded by the diversity of tones. Perhaps most important of all, in their integrating the dramatic immediacy and concentration of the short story with the sweep of sustained narrative, they reveal the carpet as containing the reconciliation of what George Steiner in *Tolstoy or Dostoyevsky* has described as antithetical if not mutually exclusive traditions of fiction. To summarize from Steiner's long list of contrarities: Faulkner, like Dostoyevsky, distrusts reason and loves paradox, distrusts total understanding and seeks to preserve some element of mystery, plunges into the labyrinth of the unnatural and the morass of the soul, and hovers on the edge of the hallucinatory, of the spectral, always vulnerable to demonic intrusions into what might prove, in the end, to have been merely a tissue of dreams. On the other hand, like Tolstoy, he is the poet of the land and of the rural setting, the man thirsting for the truth and engaging in excessive pursuit of it, the writer evoking the realness, the tangibility, the sensible entirety of concrete experience. Admittedly, to assert he is both a Tolstoy and a Dostoyevsky is a large claim but so is Faulkner's achievement.

That he was able to risk and still to achieve so much brings us full circle to the figure in the carpet, to "the very passion of his passion" that is the unifying principle for all his works. The one indispensable element that seems best to explain the characteristics identified in the preceding pages is, put most simply, the inquiring mind, that quizzical, reflective prober of persons, places, and things who simultaneously ventures into the unknown and interrogates the known. To use his own words once more: "The most important thing is insight, that is, to be—curiosity—to wonder, to mull, and to muse why it is that man does what he does." (191) It is at this point that author, character, and reader meet and see their own images reflected each in the other and in the carpet. In this we can see perhaps why the Yoknapatawpha saga remains incomplete necessarily and not simply because of Faulkner's death. For each new reader, each new critic who takes up Faulkner's task of wondering, musing, and mulling, and each new interpretation that proves less than definitive is in some sense a contribution to the saga as well as a tribute to its founder.

Conrad Aiken

William Faulkner: The Novel As Form

The famous remark made to Macaulay—"Young man, the more I consider the less can I conceive where you picked up that style"—might with advantage have been saved for Mr. William Faulkner. For if one thing is more outstanding than another about Mr. Faulkner—some readers find it so outstanding, indeed, that they never get beyond it—it is the uncompromising and almost hypnotic zeal with which he insists upon having a style, and, especially of late, the very peculiar style which he insists upon having. Perhaps to that one should add that he insists *when he remembers*—he can write straightforwardly enough when he wants to; he does so often in the best of his short stories (and they are brilliant), often enough, too, in the novels. But that *style* is what he really wants to get back to; and get back to it he invariably does.

And what a style it is, to be sure! The exuberant and tropical luxuriance of sound which Jim Europe's jazz band used to exhale, like a jungle of rank creepers and ferocious blooms taking shape before one's eyes—magnificently and endlessly intervolved, glisteningly and ophidianly in motion, coil sliding over coil, and leaf and flower forever magically interchanging—was scarcely more bewildering, in its sheer inexhaustible fecundity, than Mr. Faulkner's style. Small wonder if even the most passionate of Mr. Faulkner's admirers—among whom the present writer honors himself by enlisting—must find, with each new novel, that the first fifty pages are always the hardest, that each time one must

From The Collected Criticism of Conrad Aiken, *Oxford University Press. Reprinted by permission of Brandt & Brandt. Copyright © 1939 by Conrad Aiken. Copyright renewed 1967 by Conrad Aiken.*

learn all over again *how* to read this strangely fluid and slippery and heavily mannered prose, and that one is even, like a kind of Laocoon, sometimes tempted to give it up.

Wrestle, for example, with two very short (for Mr. Faulkner!) sentences taken from an early page of *Absalom, Absalom!* "Meanwhile, as though in inverse ratio to the vanishing voice, the invoked ghost of the man whom she could neither forgive nor revenge herself upon began to assume a quality almost of solidity, permanence. Itself circumambient and enclosed by its effluvium of hell, its aura of unregeneration, it mused (mused, thought, seemed to possess sentience as if, though dispossessed of the peace —who was impervious anyhow to fatigue—which she declined to give it, it was still irrevocably outside the scope of her hurt or harm) with that quality peaceful and now harmless and not even very attentive—the ogre-shape which, as Miss Coldfield's voice went on, resolved out of itself before Quentin's eyes the two half-ogre children, the three of them forming a shadowy background for the fourth one." Well, it may be reasonably questioned whether, on page thirteen of a novel, that little cordite bolus of suppressed reference isn't a thumping aesthetic mistake. Returned to, when one has finished the book, it may be as simple as daylight; but encountered for the first time, and no matter how often reread, it guards its enigma with the stony impassivity of the Sphinx.

Or take again from the very first page of *The Wild Palms*— Mr. Faulkner's latest novel, and certainly one of his finest—this little specimen of "exposition": "Because he had been born here, on this coast though not in this house but in the other, the residence in town, and had lived here all his life, including the four years at the State University's medical school and the two years as an intern in New Orleans where (a thick man even when young, with thick soft woman's hands, who should never have been a doctor at all, who even after the six more or less metropolitan years looked out from a provincial and insulated amazement at his classmates and fellows: the lean young men swaggering in their drill jackets on which—to him—they wore the myriad anonymous faces of the probationer nurses with a ruthless and assured braggadocio like decorations, like flower trophies) he had sickened for it." What is one to say of that—or of a sentence only a little lower on the same page which runs for thirty-three lines? Is this, somehow perverted, the influence of the later Henry James—James the Old Pretender?

In short, Mr. Faulkner's style, though often brilliant and

always interesting, is all too frequently downright bad; and it has inevitably offered an all-too-easy mark for the sharpshooting of such alert critics as Mr. Wyndham Lewis. But if it is easy enough to make fun of Mr. Faulkner's obsessions for particular words, or his indifference and violence to them, or the parrotlike mechanical mytacism (for it is really like a stammer) with which he will go on endlessly repeating such favorites as "myriad, sourceless, impalpable, outrageous, risible, profound," there is nevertheless something more to be said for his passion for overelaborate sentence structure.

Overelaborate they certainly are, baroque and involuted in the extreme, these sentences: trailing clauses, one after another, shadowily in apposition, or perhaps not even with so much connection as that; parenthesis after parenthesis, the parenthesis itself often containing one or more parentheses—they remind one of those brightly colored Chinese eggs of one's childhood, which when opened disclosed egg after egg, each smaller and subtler than the last. It is as if Mr. Faulkner, in a sort of hurried despair, had decided to try to tell us everything, absolutely everything, every last origin or source or quality or qualification, and every possible future or permutation as well, in one terrifically concentrated effort: each sentence to be, as it were, a microcosm. And it must be admitted that the practice is annoying and distracting.

It is annoying, at the end of a sentence, to find that one does not know in the least what was the subject of the verb that dangles *in vacuo*—it is distracting to have to go back and sort out the meaning, track down the structure from clause to clause, then only to find that after all it doesn't much matter, and that the obscurity was perhaps neither subtle nor important. And to the extent that one *is* annoyed and distracted, and *does* thus go back and work it out, it may be at once added that Mr. Faulkner has defeated his own ends. One has had, of course, to emerge from the stream, and to step away from it, in order properly to see it; and as Mr. Faulkner works precisely by a process of *immersion,* of hypnotizing his reader into *remaining immersed* in his stream, this occasional blunder produces irritation and failure.

Nevertheless, despite the blunders, and despite the bad habits and the willful bad writing (and willful it obviously is), the style as a whole is extraordinarily effective; the reader *does* remain immersed, *wants* to remain immersed, and it is interesting to look into the reasons for this. And at once, if one considers these queer sentences not simply by themselves, as monsters of grammar or awkwardness, but in their relation to the book as a whole, one sees a functional reason and necessity for their being as they are. They parallel in a curious and perhaps inevitable way, and not without aesthetic justification, the whole elaborate method of *deliberately withheld meaning,* of progressive and partial and delayed disclosure, which so often gives the characteristic shape to the novels themselves. It is a persistent offering of obstacles, a calculated system of screens and obtrusions, of confusions and ambiguous interpolations and delays, with one express purpose; and that purpose is simply to keep the form—and the idea—fluid and unfinished, still in motion, as it were, and unknown, until the dropping into place of the very last syllable.

What Mr. Faulkner is after, in a sense, is a *continuum.* He wants a medium without stops or pauses, a medium which is always *of the moment,* and of which the passage from moment to moment is as fluid and undetectable as in the life itself which he is purporting to give. It is all inside and underneath, or as seen from within and below; the reader must therefore be steadily *drawn in;* he must be powerfully and unremittingly hypnotized inward and downward to that image-stream; and this suggests, perhaps, a reason not only for the length and elaborateness of the sentence structure, but for the repetitiveness as well. The repetitiveness, and the steady iterative emphasis—like a kind of chanting or invocation—on certain relatively abstract words ("sonorous, latin, *vaguely* eloquent"), has the effect at last of producing, for Mr. Faulkner, a special language, a conglomerate of his own, which he uses with an astonishing virtuosity, and which, although in detailed analysis it may look shoddy, is actually for his purpose a life stream of almost miraculous adaptability. At the one extreme it is abstract, cerebral, time-and-space-obsessed, tortured and twisted, but nevertheless always with a living *pulse* in it; and at the other it can be as overwhelming in its simple vividness, its richness in the actual, as the flood scenes in *The Wild Palms.*

Obviously, such a style, especially when allied with such a method, and such a *concern* for method, must make difficulties for the reader; and it must be admitted that Mr. Faulkner does little or nothing as a rule to make his highly complex "situation" easily available or perceptible. The reader must simply make up his mind to go to work, and in a sense to coöperate; his reward being that there *is* a situation to be given shape, a meaning to be extracted, and that half the fun is precisely in watching the queer, difficult, and often so laborious, evolution of Mr. Faulkner's idea. And not so much idea, either, as form. For, like the great predecessor whom at least in this regard he so oddly resembles,

Mr. Faulkner could say with Henry James that it is practically impossible to make any real distinction between theme and form. What immoderately delights him, alike in *Sanctuary, The Sound and the Fury, As I Lay Dying, Light in August, Pylon, Absalom, Absalom!* and now again in *The Wild Palms,* and what sets him above—shall we say it firmly—all his American contemporaries, is his continuous preoccupation with the novel *as form,* his passionate concern with it, and a degree of success with it which would clearly have commanded the interest and respect of Henry James himself. The novel as revelation, the novel as slice-of-life, the novel as mere story, do not interest him: these he would say, like James again, "are the circumstances of the interest," but not the interest itself. The interest itself will be the *use* to which these circumstances are put, the degree to which they can be organized.

From this point of view, he is not in the least to be considered as a mere "Southern" writer: the "Southernness" of his scenes and characters is of little concern to him, just as little as the question whether they are pleasant or unpleasant, true or untrue. Verisimilitude—or, at any rate, *degree* of verisimilitude—he will cheerfully abandon, where necessary, if the compensating advantages of plan or tone are a sufficient inducement. The famous scene in *Sanctuary* of Miss Reba and Uncle Bud, in which a "madam" and her cronies hold a wake for a dead gangster, while the small boy gets drunk, is quite false, taken out of its context; it is not endowed with the same *kind* of actuality which permeates the greater part of the book at all. Mr. Faulkner was cunning enough to see that a two-dimensional cartoon-like statement, at this juncture, would supply him with the effect of a chorus, and without in the least being perceived as a change in the temperature of truthfulness.

That particular kind of dilution, or adulteration, of verisimilitude was both practised and praised by James: as when he blandly admitted of *In the Cage* that his central character was "too ardent a focus of divination" to be quite credible. It was defensible simply because it made possible the coherence of the whole, and was itself absorbed back into the luminous texture. It was for him a device for organization, just as the careful cherishing of "viewpoint" was a device, whether simply or in counterpoint. Of Mr. Faulkner's devices, of this sort, aimed at the achievement of complex "form," the two most constant are the manipulation of viewpoint and the use of the flash-back, or sudden shift of time-scene, forward or backward.

In *Sanctuary,* where the alternation of viewpoint is a little lawless, the complexity is given, perhaps a shade disingenuously, by violent shifts in time; a deliberate disarrangement of an otherwise straightforward story. Technically, there is no doubt that the novel, despite its fame, rattles a little; and Mr. Faulkner himself takes pains to disclaim it. But, even done with the left hand, it betrays a genius for form, quite apart from its wonderful virtuosity in other respects. *Light in August,* published a year after *Sanctuary,* repeats the same technique, that of a dislocation of time, and more elaborately; the time-shifts alternate with shifts in the viewpoint; and if the book is a failure it is perhaps because Mr. Faulkner's tendency to what is almost a hypertrophy of form is not here, as well as in the other novels, matched with the characters and the theme. Neither the person nor the story of Joe Christmas is seen fiercely enough—by its creator—to carry off that immense machinery of narrative; it would have needed another Popeye, or another Jiggs and Shumann, another Temple Drake, and for once Mr. Faulkner's inexhaustible inventiveness seems to have been at fault. Consequently what we see is an extraordinary power for form functioning relatively *in vacuo,* and existing only to sustain itself.

In the best of the novels, however—and it is difficult to choose between *The Sound and the Fury* and *The Wild Palms,* with *Absalom, Absalom!* a very close third—this tendency to hypertrophy of form has been sufficiently curbed; and it is interesting, too, to notice that in all these three (and in that remarkable *tour de force, As I Lay Dying,* as well), while there is still a considerable reliance on time-shift, the effect of richness and complexity is chiefly obtained by a very skillful fugue-like alternation of viewpoint. Fugue-like in *The Wild Palms*—and fugue-like especially, of course, in *As I Lay Dying,* where the shift is kaleidoscopically rapid, and where, despite an astonishing violence to plausibility (in the reflections, and *language* of reflection, of the characters) an effect of the utmost reality and immediateness is nevertheless produced. Fugue-like, again, in *Absalom, Absalom!* where indeed one may say the form is really circular—there is no beginning and no ending, properly speaking, and therefore no *logical* point of entrance: we must just submit, and follow the circling of the author's interest, which turns a light inward towards the centre, but every moment from a new angle, a new point of view. The story unfolds, therefore, now in one color of light, now in another, with references backward and forward: those that refer forward being necessarily, for the moment, blind. What is complete in Mr. Faulkner's pattern, *a priori,* must nevertheless remain *in-*

complete for us until the very last stone is in place; what is "real," therefore, at one stage of the unfolding, or from one point of view, turns out to be "unreal" from another; and we find that one among other things with which we are engaged is the fascinating sport of trying to separate truth from legend, watching the growth of legend from truth, and finally reaching the conclusion that the distinction is itself false.

Something of the same sort is true also of *The Sound and the Fury*—and this, with its massive four-part symphonic structure, is perhaps the most beautifully *wrought* of the whole series, and an indubitable masterpiece of what James loved to call the "fictive art." The joinery is flawless in its intricacy; it is a novelist's novel—a whole textbook on the craft of fiction in itself, comparable in its way to *What Maisie Knew* or *The Golden Bowl.*

But if it is important, for the moment, to emphasize Mr. Faulkner's genius for form, and his continued exploration of its possibilities, as against the usual concern with the violence and dreadfulness of his themes—though we might pause to remind carpers on this score of the fact that the best of Henry James is precisely that group of last novels which so completely concerned themselves with moral depravity—it is also well to keep in mind his genius for invention, whether of character or episode. The inventiveness is of the richest possible sort—a headlong and tumultuous abundance, an exuberant generosity and vitality, which makes most other contemporary fiction look very pale and chaste indeed. It is an unforgettable gallery of portraits, whether character or caricature, and all of them endowed with a violent and immediate vitality.

"He is at once"—to quote once more from James—"one of the most corrupt of writers and one of the most naïf, the most mechanical and pedantic, and the fullest of *bonhomie* and natural impulse. He is one of the finest of artists and one of the coarsest. Viewed in one way, his novels are ponderous, shapeless, overloaded; his touch is graceless, violent, barbarous. Viewed in another, his tales have more color, more composition, more grasp of the reader's attention than any others. [His] style would demand a chapter apart. It is the least simple style, probably, that was ever written; it bristles, it cracks, it swells and swaggers; but it is a perfect expression of the man's genius. Like his genius, it contains a certain quantity of everything, from immaculate gold to flagrant dross. He was a very bad writer, and yet unquestionably he was a very great writer. We may say briefly, that in so far as his method was an instinct it was successful, and that in so far as it was a theory it was a failure. But both in instinct and in theory he had the aid of an immense force of conviction. His imagination warmed to its work so intensely that there was nothing his volition could not impose upon it. Hallucination settled upon him, and he believed anything that was necessary in the circumstances."

That passage, from Henry James's essay on Balzac, is almost word for word, with scarcely a reservation, applicable to Mr. Faulkner. All that is lacking is Balzac's greater *range* of understanding and tenderness, his greater freedom from special preoccupations. For this, one would hazard the guess that Mr. Faulkner has the gifts—and time is still before him.

William Van O'Connor

Rhetoric in Southern Writing: Faulkner

Faulkner's rhetoric has several sources: it is indebted to Tennyson and to Swinburne, to the elegance of *le fin de siècle,* to the Ciceronian periods of Southern oratory, and to a Southern folk tradition that is anti-grammatical and colorful. Perhaps his major styles can be classified as "high rhetoric" and as "folk language." The two styles meet in *The Hamlet,* and there are varieties of the folk language in most of his books. When people speak of Faulkner's rhetoric, however, they commonly mean the "high rhetoric."

Millar McClure, writing in the *Queen's Quarterly* (Autumn, 1956), says: "Faulkner's prose has an archaic sound, like a hunter's horn." That is the best characterization of it I have read. Faulkner's prose has a nineteenth century quality, it belongs to a different world from the present.

Perhaps the simplest way of examining the high rhetoric is to read and then analyze a characteristic sentence. The sentence is from "The Bear":

> It was as if the boy had already divined what his senses and intellect had not encompassed yet: that doomed wilderness whose edges were being constantly and punily gnawed at by men with plows and axes who feared it because it was wilderness, men myriad and nameless even to one another in the land where the old bear had earned a name, and through which ran not even a mortal beast but an anachronism indomitable and invincible out of an old dead time, a phantom, epitome and apotheosis of the old life which the little puny humans swarmed and hacked at in fury of abhorrence and fear like pygmies about the ankles of a drowsing elephant; —the old bear, solitary, indomitable, and alone; widowered, childless and absolved of mortality—old Priam reft of his old wife and outlived all his sons.

Reprinted with permission from The Georgia Review, *XII (Spring, 1958), 83–86.*

First, there is the suspension of meaning in the long sentence, there are colons, semicolons, and dashes (sometimes there are parentheses); the sentence is a small self-contained world. Second, there is the now famous vocabulary: *divined, encompassed, doomed, myriad, nameless, anachronism, indomitable, invincible, phantom, apotheosis, abhorrence, absolved*—words that evoke an older morality and recall an older order. Third, there is a reference to a tragic or noble event in an older romantic literature—"old Priam." Fourth, there is the negative followed by a positive, usually, not this nor this but this; in this sentence, it is "and through which ran *not* even a mortal beast *but* an anachronism indomitable and invincible. . . ." Fifth, there is repetition: "*solitary*, indomitable, and *alone*." Sixth, there is poetic extension of meaning brought about by an unexpected word, "absolved of mortality," whereas one expected "freed from" or "escaped from." Seventh, there is the metaphor the vehicle of which is foreign to the subject under discussion, but which sheds a light on that subject: thus the relationship of the men to the bear is likened to pygmies troubling a drowsy elephant. And lastly, there is Faulkner's indifference to standard structures—"reft of his old wife and outlived all his sons."

There are several other characteristic devices which are not found in this passage: the use of paradox, as in the oxymoron "roaring silence"; the piling up of adjectives as in the phrase "passionate tragic ephemeral loves of adolescence" (leaving out of commas of course adds to the dream-like quality, the being above time and space that the true work of art sometimes achieves); the running of two words together (after the manner of Joyce and Cummings), such as "allembracing" and "eunuchmountebank"; and the liking for hyphenated words, as with "rodent-scavengered tomb," "smoke-colored twilight," or better, this sentence: "It (the talking, the telling) seemed (to him, to Quentin) to partake of that logic—and reason-flouting quality upon which it must depend to move the dreamer (verisimilitude) to credulity—horror or pleasure or amazement—depends as completely upon a formal recognition of an acceptance of elapsed and yet-elapsing time as music or a printed tale."

What do we have thus far in the way of devices? We have

1. the long sentence, with colons, semicolons, dashes, and parentheses
2. the vocabulary that evokes an older morality and a realm of high romance

3. the allusions to romantic episodes in history and in literature
4. the sentence that employs a negative or series of negatives followed by a positive
5. the use of synonyms for the purpose of repetition
6. a symbolist or poetic extension of the meaning of words
7. the reaching out for a metaphor or a simile the "vehicle" of which is foreign to the subject being discussed
8. breaking with standard grammatical forms; sometimes solecisms
9. the use of paradox
10. the piling up of adjectives
11. the merging of two words into one word
12. the use of hyphenated words

For many writers the paragraph, or the chapter, or even the over-all argument or thesis is the chief unit of composition. For Faulkner the chief unit is the sentence. His ideal, as certain sections in *Requiem for a Nun* suggest, would be a booklength sentence. His public statements and short speeches show that Faulkner is not a gifted expository writer, and he seems incapable of developing a thesis slowly or subtly. Faulkner's sentences evoke, they do not state. Perhaps I should qualify this argument to the extent of saying the sentence is the chief unit in those books that most depend upon the high style. The parallel phrases, the repetitions, the circling of the subject, or the piling up of adjectives— everything contributes to a self-contained and static world. Faulkner's sentences are spatial rather than analytical.

One is likely to think of Faulkner as having a "voice," just as one thinks of James as having a voice. Faulkner's world lives because the voice evokes it for us, just as James' world lives in the Master's polite, intelligent telling. There is, of course, a distinction. All of James' characters talk Jamesian English. Faulkner's characters have identities apart from as well as in relation to the "voice." Sometimes the "voice" takes over or heightens a character's speech, and sometimes it is a "chorus" saying what the events at the front of the stage signify. We may look at the following example, the close of Chapter IV of *Absalom, Absalom!*. Quentin is imagining the final encounter between Henry Sutpen and his brother Charles Bon:

They faced one another on the two gaunt horses, two men, young, not yet in the world, not yet breathed over it long enough, to be old but with old eyes, with unkempt hair and faces gaunt and weathered as if cast by some spartan and even niggard hand from bronze, in worn and patched gray weathered now to the color of dead leaves, the one with the tarnished braid of an officer, the other plain of cuff, the pistol lying yet across the saddle bow unaimed, the two faces calm, the voices not even raised: *Don't you pass the shadow of this post, this branch, Charles;* and *I am going to pass it, Henry.*

Almost all of the characteristics of Faulkner's high rhetoric are here. It is Faulkner's "voice," not Quentin's. It is Faulkner's evocation over the shoulder of Quentin. The passage that immediately follows, however, the speech of Mr. Compson recalling Wash Jones' reporting the murder, comes as an electrifying contrast:

... and then Wash Jones sitting that saddleless mule before Miss Rosa's gate, shouting her name into the sunny and peaceful quiet of the street, saying, "Air you Rosie Coldfield? Then you better come on out yon. Henry has done shot that durn French feller. Kilt him dead as a beef."

Compson's idiom is his own, and Wash Jones' idiom is decidedly his—and they release the reader from the hypnotic world created by the "voice." Or perhaps one should say they enlarge or extend the world created by the "voice."

Ratliffe's speech is probably the purest example of the folk style. This is a passage from *The Hamlet:*

I did, that is, because Ab was laying out in the wagon bed by then, flat on his back with the rain popping him in the face and me on the slat driving now and watching the shiny black horse just turning into a bay horse. Because I was just eight then, and me and Ab had done all our horse trading up and down that lane that run past his lot. So I just drove under the first roof I come to and shaken Ab awake.

Many of Faulkner's characters talk a variety of folk language, including some, like Gavin Stevens, with university degrees. Sometimes they shift from standard to folk usages and back again in a single conversation.

Although they are far from fully accounting for Faulkner's success as a fiction writer, these styles, the high style and the folk style, do account for much of his greatness. There are innumerable passages that would serve very well as set pieces for anthologies. He has always been able to use language as a virtuoso—but if this helps to account for his genius it also helps to account for his failures, especially his more recent failures, *The Fable* and *The Town*. In the former, the high style creates a world out of words, a world that seems hypnotized and bemused by the sounds that went into its making. In the latter, each of the narrators is a cracker-barrel philosopher, pleased as all hell with his shrewd and comic folk idiom. In each book character and dramatized incident have been sacrificed to Faulkner's style, to the voice of the high rhetoric, and to the color of the folk language.

Robert Penn Warren

Faulkner: Past and Future

Faulkner began writing . . . in the full tide of the Coolidge Boom, but the crash had long since come—in October 1929—by the time *l'affaire Faulkner* was presented to general attention with the publication, in 1931, of *Sanctuary*. Certainly, the assumptions and tone of Faulkner's work would have seemed irrelevant in the context of the Boom; in the context of the Depression they often seemed, not irrelevant, but inimical.

In the great objective world, in a context of human suffering, issues of the most profound social, political, and moral importance were being fought out, and it was only natural that practical men, if they happened to have read or have heard of Faulkner, should regard his work as merely a pathological vision happily distant from serious concerns—unless, of course, it could be used as evidence of the need for an enlarged PWA program or free shoes in that barefoot world. It was, as I have said, only natural that practical men, if they read Faulkner at all, should have read him in this spirit, and the fact is not significant.

What is, however, significant—and significant in a way far transcending the fate of the work of Faulkner—is that, by and large, the world of "impractical" men, of intellectuals, betrayed its trust by trying to be "practical," resigned its function of criticizing and interpreting the demands of the practical world, and often became a comic parody—comic because dealing with the shadow not the substance of power and action—of the world of practicality. What could not be converted in a mechanical, schematic, and immediate way into an accepted formula for social action was

From Robert Penn Warren, Editor, FAULKNER: A Collection of Critical Essays © *1966. Reprinted by permission of Prentice-Hall, Inc., Englewood Cliffs, New Jersey.*

interpreted as "reactionary," "decadent," "gothic," "fascist," or merely "Southern."

All these elements were, in fact, in Faulkner's work. The work was certainly Southern to the bone, and it was easy to find elements in Southern life, and in Faulkner's work, which, taken in isolation, might suggest the word *fascist,* and all the rest. For instance, the delusions of a Gail Hightower might provide the compost for breeding fascism, and there was, thirty-odd years ago, as now, many a Percy Grimm in the South, a type not too unlike a certain kind of fascist bully-boy. But the mere presence, in isolation, is not what is important. What is important is the context, the dialectic, in which such elements appear. We have only to look at the role of Hightower in *Light in August,* or to remember that Faulkner prided himself on Percy Grimm as his invention of a Nazi Stormtrooper. Or we may set the distortions some critics made of the role of Negro characters in Faulkner's work over against the role Negroes actually play in the work. The fact that meaning is always a matter of relation should be clear to anyone—though it was not clear to certain well-intentioned men who had sacrificed their intelligence in the cause of what they regarded as virtue.

This is not to say that Faulkner was the victim of a conspiracy among card-carrying, or even fellow-traveling, book reviewers. A climate can be more lethal than a conspiracy, and the climate was that of para-Marxist neo-naturalism, with the doctrine of art-as-illustration—debates concerning which we can find embalmed, for example, in the proceedings of the American Writers' Congress. Since such "leftism" had become intellectually chic, the new attitudes were assimilated with no pain and little reflection by college professors, ladies' clubs, news-minded literary editors, and book reviewers who a few short years before might have attacked Faulkner merely because he was dirty and not very optimistic. In the new context, the combination of tragic intensity, ribald and rambunctious comedy, violence and pathology, Negro field hands and Mississippi aristocrats, old-fashioned rhetoric and new-fangled time shifts, symbolism and obscurity, amounted to outrage—and probably to fascism.

Even if *Sartoris, The Sound and the Fury,* and *As I Lay Dying* were commercial failures, a certain number of reviewers had recognized talent, but as the new decade took shape, the talent, even when recognized, was often recognized more grudgingly—or even with the sense that the presence of talent compounded the original outrage. This clearly was not a literature in tune with the New Deal, the new post office art, the new social conscience, the new

Moscow trials, or the new anything. It was, simply, new: that is, created. And in some circles, at all times, for a thing to be truly created, is to be outrageous.[1]

The literary criticism of the Depression slipped without any grinding of gears into that of the War period. The literary criticism of the War period, stimulated by the War in Spain, antedated Pearl Harbor by several years. The atmosphere of war simply added a new element, and a new justification, to the attitudes of the Depression, and added to the list of writers to be taken by men of good will as irrelevant, or inimical, to social progress. As the shadow of war grew, critics more and more found reprehensible all literary work that emphasized lags between our professions of national faith and our performance. In fact, it sometimes seemed that, with the pressure of events, the rise of patriotism, and the exigencies of propaganda, it was less important to clean up our messes than to sweep them under the rug. If America was the temple, as well as the arsenal, of democracy, it should be presented, for the sake of a higher truth and by a higher law, in the most effective way possible, with *son et lumière*—appropriate music and strategically placed floodlights for tourists, who were to be admitted to the spectacle only after the vulgar, factual glare of day had been mercifully withdrawn.

In a way somewhat unfair to what he actually said, Archibald MacLeish's essay "The Irresponsibles" was generally taken as the

[1] For the record, and for their honor, it must be pointed out that some of the critics most firmly grounded in, and best informed about, Marxism did not fall into the trap. For instance, that brilliant and seminal critic, Kenneth Burke, the whole thrust of whose work was counter to such bigotry, and who, in 1939, after war had begun, remarked in a letter to the present writer that one could still learn more about men "from tropes than from tropisms." And there is Malcolm Cowley, the differences in whose background and philosophical and political assumptions did not prevent the long struggle of imagination which led to his editing of *The Portable Faulkner.*

Some documentation of this struggle is to be found in the series of reviews *(Pylon, Absalom, Absalom!, The Wild Palms, The Hamlet, Go Down, Moses)* which Cowley did in *The New Republic.* Cowley's main objection is repeated several times—that there is some sort of split in Faulkner, "a lack of proportion between stimulus and response," as he says of *Pylon,* and in other terms, about *Absalom, Absalom!,* which, he says, falls "short of the powerful mood it might have achieved." In fact, even as late as 1940, in reviewing *The Hamlet,* Cowley says that "one admires the author while feeling that most of his books are Gothic ruins, impressive only by moonlight." By 1942, however, in reviewing *Go Down, Moses,* he can say that "there is no other American writer who has been so consistently misrepresented by his critics, including myself." Then after an attack on the views of Maxwell Geismar and Granville Hicks, he says Faulkner is "after Hemingway and perhaps Dos Passos, the most considerable novelist of this generation."

prime statement of this attitude. But MacLeish did see and deplore a split between literature and what he regarded as political responsibility—an attitude which he put more precisely in another essay "Post-War Writers and Pre-War Readers"[2] where he specifically condemned Barbusse, Ford, Hemingway, Dos Passos, Remarque, and Aldington because "what they wrote, however noble it may have been as literature, however true to them as a summary of their personal experience, was disastrous as education for a generation which would be obliged to face the threat of fascism in its adult years."[3] Faulkner, of course, became—or rather, long before, had become—the most obvious target for this attitude; and the notion that he was a liability for which American patriots should apologize, persisted even in the editorial in which the *New York Times* commented on the Nobel Prize:

> His [Faulkner's] field of vision is concentrated on a society that is too often vicious, depraved, decadent, corrupt. Americans must fervently hope that the award by a Swedish jury and the enormous vogue of Faulkner's works in Latin America and on the European Continent, especially in France, does not mean that foreigners admire him because he gives them the picture of American life they believe to be typical and true. There has been too much of that feeling lately, again especially in France. Incest and rape may be common pastimes in Faulkner's "Jefferson, Miss." but they are not elsewhere in the United States.

To return to the time of the coming of World War II, the notion that Faulkner's complicated techniques were somehow asso-

[2] *The New Republic,* June 10, 1940.

[3] There was a kind of comic justice in the fact that MacLeish was occasionally tarred with his own brush. Oscar Cargill, in a book called *Intellectual America: Ideas on the March* (1941) did not forgive him, despite "The Irresponsibles," and pilloried him among those he calls the "Decadents"—a group including Eliot, Hart Crane, and Pound. Cargill admitted that it was "hard to find four other poets with equal importance, but went on to say that, "Like Naturalism, Decadence, has exerted an enfeebling influence on American character. . . ." "The fall of France," he adds elsewhere, "was brought about in part (as Mr. MacLeish must realize) by decadent intellectualism."

This book, *Intellectual America,* is undoubtedly one of the curiosities of our (or any) literature. It also has a less morbid value as a reference book, in that it encyclopedically commemorates, in a naked and simple form, all the clichés of thought and expression of a decade. Mr. Cargill desperately wanted literature to serve the good of mankind, but having not the foggiest notion of what literature is, he couldn't easily figure out what good it might serve—not any good from the "Naturalists," nor the "Decadents," nor the "Primitivists," nor the "Intelligentsia," (with a sub-head for "Modern Cynicism") nor the "Freudians." Among those Polonian (and Procrustean) categories Faulkner is crammed among the "Primitivists."

ciated with reprehensible content anticipated a line of criticism brought to bear on Pound's poetry after his capture and imprisonment. Back in 1940, Percy Boynton had commented on such a connection in Faulkner's work by affirming that "the technique is simple and the content more lucid in those tales which have the greater normality," and becomes "more intricate and elusive in the tales of abnormality," and that "technique becomes a compensation for content as content sinks in the social scale." By this line of reasoning the prose of the famous corn cob scene would, of course, make that of *Finnegan's Wake* look like a selection from *The Bobbsey Twins.*[4]

Faulkner's trouble with the patriots was compounded by two other factors. First, he had no truck with any obvious programs for social salvation. Steinbeck and Caldwell, though they both showed abuses and degradation in American life, showed them with a diagnosis and the hint of a quick cure that was fashionable in the reviewing trade. Second, Faulkner was Southern. Of course, Wolfe was Southern too; but nobody ever took him for a fascist; he showed none of the dark ambivalences of Quentin Compson, off at Harvard, telling the story of Sutpen to the innocent Canadian. Furthermore, Wolfe hymned America in terms reminiscent of, it was said, Whitman.

A little later, with the War well started, *The Valley of Decision,* by Marcia Davenport, was widely hailed as a major contribution to literature and to the war effort. A little later still, *Strange Fruit,* by Lillian Smith, in the moment of a new conscience on the race question stimulated by the need for black factory hands and black troops and by A. Philip Randolph's March-on-Washington movement, was received with hosannahs by a chorus of critics led by Eleanor Roosevelt. By this time Faulkner's most recent book, *Go Down, Moses,* which also had something to do with conscience and the race question, was forgotten, and by 1945 all seventeen of his books were out of print.

The great watershed for Faulkner's reputation in the United States is usually, and quite correctly, taken to be the publication of *The Portable Faulkner* in 1946. Several factors contributed to the effect of the *Portable.* First, Cowley's Introduction, developing but substantially modifying a line of interpretation originally suggested, in 1939, by George Marion O'Donnell, persuasively in-

---

[4] In . . . *Love and Death in the American Novel* . . . Leslie Fiedler uses the same kind of argument about style in passages where Faulkner writes of characters of mixed Negro and white blood.

sisted on the significant coherence of Faulkner's work taken as a whole. Second, the selection itself was made with taste and cunning to support the thesis. Third, the fact that the reputation of Cowley himself as associated with the "left wing," as critic and as editor of *The New Republic* (in which *The Sound and the Fury* had been reviewed, though not by Cowley, under the head "Signifying Nothing"), gave a certain piquancy, and in some circles, an air of authority and respectability to his estimate of Faulkner. Fourth, the time was ripe.

By 1946 the climate had changed—if not for the better, at least for a difference. With Hitler dead in his bunker and the Duce hung by his heels at the filling station in Milan, and with the marriage of American liberalism and Joseph Stalin running on the rocks, a new kind of idiocy became fashionable and raced forward to fulfillment in Joe McCarthy; and Faulkner no longer served the old function of scapegoat of all work. He had survived—endured, in fact—and was part of the landscape, like a hill or a tree.

I do not know what force the college classrooms of the country exert in making or breaking literary reputations, but in the period of the late thirties and early forties, when professors of American literature and of the then new-fangled American Studies were often inclined to speak of Steinbeck's *In Dubious Battle* and of Howard Fast's *Citizen Tom Paine* in the tones of hushed reverence once reserved for the works of Sophocles, Faulkner had received short shrift. After the War, with the horde of returning GI's, the process backfired. As one GI put it to me, "I been robbed!" He reported that in the good university where he had pernoctated before the call to arms, his class in American literature had dedicated six weeks to *The Grapes of Wrath* and thirty minutes to Faulkner, thirty minutes being long enough to allow the professor to document from *A Rose for Emily,* the only work investigated, that Faulkner was a cryptofascist. Such young men immersed themselves in the work of Faulkner with ferocious attention. As far as I could determine, they had little of that kind of romantic disillusion that was reputed to have been common after World War I. They were motivated, rather, by a disgust for simple, schematic, two-dimensional views of the world. Many of them had had, first-hand, a shocking acquaintance with the depths and paradoxes of experience, and now literary renderings that did not honor their experience were not for them. Furthermore, as a corollary, they, having been caught in the great dehumanizing machine of war, were forced to reflect on their own relation to the modern world, not in terms of political and social arrangements, but in terms of identity itself. That is, they found in the works of Faulkner and in the method of his works something that corresponded to, and validated, their own experience.

Returning GI's did not, however, exclusively constitute the new and expanding readership of Faulkner, though their view of the world may have had something in common with that of some nonmilitary citizens of the United States, or with that of the Japanese, French, and Italians, military and nonmilitary, who took his fiction to their hearts. It can, perhaps, be plausibly argued that Faulkner is one of the few contemporary fiction writers—perhaps the only American—whose work is to any considerable degree concerned with the central issues of our time, who really picks at the scab of our time, in the way that, in varying degrees of intensity and scale, Melville, Dostoevsky, Kafka, Conrad, Proust, Eliot, Yeats, and Camus, also do.

In thinking of such a question, we must remember that being topical and being central are two very different things. In the 1930s —as now—there were battalions of writers in the United States who programmatically tried to will themselves into tune with the Zeitgeist. The trouble was that, almost to a man, they confused the Zeitgeist with current newspaper headlines and lead reviews in the Sunday book sections. The Zeitgeist may speak through the headlines, just as it may speak through a new metric or a theory of corporate structure; but we cannot therefore assume that the headlines *are* the Zeitgeist. Rather, some writer who most obviously seems to be in tune with the Zeitgeist may be merely caught in a superficial eddy of history, which often, as Melville, in "The Conflict of Convictions," puts it, "spins against the way it drives." By the same token, the writer who seems alienated and withdrawn may appear, in the light of history, as central. For instance, at the moment when Milton, blind, defeated and obscure, was composing *Paradise Lost,* would anybody have thought him central?

Perhaps what the returning GI's found in Faulkner is what had drawn other readers, too. Perhaps the blind, blank, dehumanized and dehumanizing, depersonalized and depersonalizing modern war is the appropriate metaphor for our age—or for one aspect of our age—and paraphrasing Clausewitz, we may say that war is merely an extension of our kind of peace. In that case, we are all GI's, and any reader may come, in mufti, to Faulkner's work with the same built-in questions as the GI of 1946, seeking the same revelatory images of experience. Perhaps the images of violence, in which Faulkner's work abounds, are, to adapt a famous remark by Poe, not of the South but of the soul; and perhaps their Southernness has such a deep appeal because this order of violence, with the teasing charm of antiquity, is associated with the assertion of, or the quest for, selfhood, the discovery of a role, or the declaration of a value, in the context of anonymous violence or blankness. Perhaps all the images in Faulkner's work of the mystic marriage of the hunter and the hunted have a meaning more metaphysical than anthropological; and all the images of isolation, self-imposed by a wrong relation to nature or to history, or visited blindly on the individual, are to be taken as images of the doom that we all, increasingly in our time, must struggle against; and the images of Southern alienation are only images of Everyman facing one of the possibilities in his world. Perhaps we see in the agonies, longings, and nobilities of the unimportant people like Charlotte Rittenmeyer or the convict of *Wild Palms,* like Joe Christmas, like Ruby of *Sanctuary,* like Dilsey, or even like the idiot Snopes, some image of the meaningfulness of the individual effort and experience over against the machine of the world.

It is not only the implications of the objective dramatizations in Faulkner's work — character and situation — which have attracted readers. The sense of the work's being a subjective dramatization has been there too — the sense that the world created so powerfully represents a projection of an inner experience of the author somehow not too different from one the reader might know all too well. Faulkner has a remarkable ear for speech — either in dialogue or in the long narrative monologue, like that of Jason, for instance, or that of Ratliff in "Spotted Horses," the early version of the horse auction scene of *The Hamlet.* But generally Faulkner's narratives are sustained not by such reported, or ventriloquist, voices, but by a single dominant voice[5] — the highly personal style which, for better or worse, seems to be the index of the subjective drama, and which guarantees to the reader that the story is truly alive in the deepest way. As Albert Thilbaudet says of Proust, the tide of his sentences carries with it as it advances the creative élan that gives it life; or as Monique Nathan puts it in her book about Faulkner, there is something "almost liturgical" in the function of his style. And we might add that, to take the Aristotelian terms, a novel of Faulkner combines the drama (or narrative) and the dithyramb, the latter being the per-

[5] The transfer of the horse auction scene from Ratliff to the "voice" in the novel affords a beautiful case history of this point.

sonal medium in which the impersonal renderings of experience
are sustained.

The mask-like, taciturn and withdrawn quality of Faulkner
the man, and the impersonality of his fiction, compared, for example, with that of Wolfe, Hemingway, or Fitzgerald, seems, para-
doxically, to attest to a deep, secret involvement, to the possibility
of a revelation which the reader might wrest from the Delphic
darkness. Malraux has hinted at this inner involvement, surmising
that Faulkner would often imagine his scenes before imagining
his characters, and that a work would not be for him "une histoire"
the development of which would determine situation, but quite the
contrary, springing from the encounter of faceless characters unknown to him, shrouded figures charged with possibility. If I read
Malraux aright, he is implying that the germ of a work might lie
in such an archetypal scene—a flash—in which all else, story
and character, would be hidden; the scene being a living, intimate
metaphor direct from the author's depth. There is some support
for Malraux's surmise in the fact that *The Sound and the Fury,*
according to Faulkner's testimony, developed from the vision of a
little girl's muddy drawers, and *Light in August,* from the vision of
"a young woman, pregnant, walking along a strange road." The
relation of the author to such a vision is directly personal, springing unbidden, as I have said, from the depth; the vision like a poul-
tice, draws the characters and the action out of him. To put it another way, the vision, in the first place, is only the projection of,
and focus for, that subjective drama which, though distorted
beyond all recognition, may become the story, the objective drama
that will carry the mystic burden of the secret involvement from
which it springs.

It would be misleading to imply that there is now a massive
unanimity of praise for Faulkner's work. Over the years various
kinds of attack have been mounted against it, but the most important line of adverse criticism now with us is that Faulkner is basically confused in thought and unclear in style. The best advertised
exponents of this view appeared a number of years ago, one being
Clifton Fadiman, in his review of *Absalom, Absalom!* in *The New
Yorker* in 1936, and the other being Alfred Kazin, whose *On
Native Ground* appeared in 1942. Though Kazin recognized Faulkner's powers of invention, and stylistic and technical resourceful-
ness, he complained that Faulkner has "no primary and design-
like conception of the South, that his admiration and acceptance
and disgust operated together in his mind"; that "as a participant

in the communal myth of the South's tradition and decline, Faulkner was curiously dull, furiously commonplace, and often meaningless, suggesting some ambiguous irresponsibility and exasperated sullenness of mind, some distant atrophy or indifference"; that his work does not "spring from a conscious and procreative criticism of society"; that there is a "gap between the deliberation of his effects, the intensity of his every conception, and the besetting and depressing looseness, the almost sick passivity, of his basic meaning and purpose"; and that his complicated technique "seems to spring from an obscure and profligate confusion, a manifest absence of purpose, rather than from an elaborate but coherent aim."

In all fairness it should be said that in later years Kazin's attitude has mellowed greatly, a change of which I first became aware at a round table on Faulkner at Columbia University, provoked by the award of the Nobel Prize, where Kazin eloquently defended Faulkner's work against the old charge of being primarily a neurotic manifestation. Even so, though more willing, with the years, to recognize the importance of Faulkner's work and to be more lavish of compliments, Kazin is still distressed by what he terms Faulkner's "attempt to will his powerful material into a kind of harmony that it does not really possess." This remark appears in an excellent essay on *Light in August,* which Kazin is willing to call "great" (the essay appearing as a book entitled *Twelve Original Essays on Great American Novels*), but which he says is "somewhat more furious in expression than meaningful in content." This essay does offer a brilliant and important treatment of Joe Christmas as the "incarnation of 'man,'"—but at the same time finds him "compelling rather than believable." So, here reappears, though in a more sympathetic and guarded form, the same objection that had appeared in *On Native Ground:* the objection that there is a gap between the talent ("compelling") and the meaning ("believable"), that the polarities and contradictions of the material have not been "really" put into "harmony."

There is no clear and objective way to settle this question, any more than there is to settle the similar question raised by E. M. Forster's charge, in *Abinger Harvest,* that Conrad "is misty in the middle as well as at the edges, that the secret casket contains a vapor rather than a jewel." In such cases, we usually come to a matter of temperament, training, and cast of mind. What many readers prize in Faulkner's work is often the fact of the polarities, contradictions, and inharmonious elements which they would take to be "really" inherent in life deeply regarded and which offer the creative spirit its most fruitful challenge—though the challenge is to a battle that can never be finally won. Kazin, however, would still seem to imply that the process of creation is much more deductive, that it should spring from an "elaborate but coherent aim," that good work should "spring from a conscious and procreative criticism of society . . . from some absolute knowledge."

Clearly, "absolute knowledge" is not what Faulkner's work springs from, or pretends to achieve. It springs from, shall we say, a need—not a program or even an intention or a criticism of society—to struggle with the painful incoherences and paradoxes of life, and with the contradictory and often unworthy impulses and feelings in the self, in order to achieve meaning; but to struggle, in the awareness that meaning, if achieved, will always rest in perilous balance, and that the great undergirding and overarching meaning of life is in the act of trying to create meaning through struggle. To a mind that is basically schematic, deductive, and rationalistic, with an appetite for "absolute knowledge," such a writer as Faulkner is bound to generate difficulties and severe discontents. But the service which a critic with such a cast of mind may do is important; he may set bounds to enthusiasms, may drive readers to define what kinds (if any) of resolution and unity have actually been achieved, may drive readers to try to determine how much of what they admire is actually there in a given work and how much is a projection of their own needs and prejudices.

But a critic, like a writer, must finally take the risk of his own formulations—this, despite the favorite delusion of all critics, who are after all human beings, that their formulations are somehow exempt from the vicissitudes of life which the novel or poem must endure. As a matter of fact, the moment a critic sets pen to paper, or finger to keyboard, the novel or poem itself becomes the silent and sleepless critic of the critic, and it is just possible that the split which Kazin sees between talent and achievement in Faulkner, between furious expression and meaningless content, indicates not so much a split in the thing criticized as in the critic— a split in the critic himself between a mind, with the laudable appetite for "absolute knowledge," and an artistic sensibility which allows for the sincere but troubling appreciation of "talent," "technique," and "effects," and for isolated instances of pathos and drama.

I have referred to Kazin because he puts the argument against Faulkner more fully and effectively than any other critic. But the argument is an old one. It had appeared, troublingly, in Cowley's early reviews. It had appeared in Wyndham Lewis' savage and funny essay, "The Moralist with a Corn-Cob," in his *Men Without Art* (1934). There Lewis has good sport at the expense of Faulkner's style, but finds little beyond the façade of "ill-selected words." The characters, he says, "are as heavily energized as the most energetic could wish," but they are "energized and worked-up to no purpose—all 'signifying nothing,'" and the "destiny" or "doom" behind Faulkner's fiction is merely a fraudulent device for operating the puppets. Sean O'Faolain, more than twenty years later, takes the same line—the style is inflated and inaccurate, is fustian, not the "artist's meaningful language" but the "demagogue's careless, rhetorical and often meaningless language," and all of this is an index to an "inward failure to focus clearly," to a lack of intelligence, to an inner "daemon" rather than a proper subject, to "ideals that he can vaguely feel but never express."

Somewhat more recently as an example of a somewhat different line of criticism, we may take an essay by Walter J. Slatoff, "The Edge of Order: The Pattern of Faulkner's Rhetoric," which maintains that Faulkner's "temperamental response rather than any theories of ideas and particular torments" are what the author "trusts to produce order in his art"—that the art represents an overabundance of oxymorons, contradictions, oppositions, polarities, which remain unresolved, that, in treating Isaac McCaslin, Faulkner has made "the choice which he can rarely resist, and which . . . seriously limits his stature, the choice not to choose." I have said that this line of criticisms, which in various forms not infrequently appears, is different from that of Lewis, Kazin, and O'Faolain: but it is different only in approach, for in the end it amounts to much the same thing, turgidity of style and inner meaninglessness, as temperament or obsession or daemon takes over the role of ideas, ideals, brains, intelligence, or "absolute knowledge."

I must refer to one more variant, and an important one, of the criticism that Faulkner's work lacks intelligence and meaning. This is the view that he has not been able to understand the nature of our age and therefore is not relevant for us who live in it. Faulkner, according to Norman Podhoretz,[6] who best exemplifies this line of attack, has entirely missed the Enlightenment, with its "qualities of reasonableness, moderation, compromise, tolerance,

[6] "William Faulkner and the Problem of War: His Fable of Faith," . . . [*Commentary*, Sept., 1954].

sober choice—in short, the anti-apocalyptic style of life brought
into the modern world by the middle class." Faulkner "doesn't
even hate" the middle class "accurately," his Jason being as much
a creature of compulsion as Quentin, without "sober choice," etc.
Having missed the Enlightenment and not understanding the
middle class, Faulkner really lacks a sense of history, and therefore cannot record the real shock of change in modernity. For
instance, what has the "Glory celebrated in Yoknapatawpha got
to do with the Korean War[7] . . . a war uninspiring, nay meaningless, to the Yoknapatawpha mind, and thrilling only to children of
the Enlightenment who understand its moral sublimity?" Faulkner
has, in *A Fable* (and we are given to understand in his other works
too) taken refuge in "Larger Considerations," and an apocalyptic
view of life and literary style, because he fails to understand the
real issues and values of modernity, including the sublimity of the
Korean War.

Podhoretz's essay was prompted by *A Fable,* and I must say
that I agree with him that this novel is, finally, a colossal failure
and a colossal bore, and that it is as confused in conception as in
execution. What I do not agree with is that it represents merely
an extension of Faulkner's work. It may well be true—and I assume that it is true—that Faulkner intended *A Fable* to be an
extension, and a generalization of the *meaning,* of his previous
work, and to serve as a basis of exegesis for his work. And it is true
that themes and ideas do come over from the past. But there is a
difference, and a crucial one, between *A Fable* and the other work
(with the exception of *Intruder in the Dust,* of which I shall speak
later). *A Fable* is abstractly conceived; it is an idea deductively
worked out—and at critical moments, blurred out. By the very
absoluteness of the failure, however, *A Fable* indicates, not so
much the limit of, as the nature of, Faulkner's success. Faulkner,
like Antaeus, could fight only with his feet on the ground—on
home ground; he had to work toward meaning through the complexity and specificity of a literal world in which he knew his way
about, as a man knows his way about his own house without thinking how he gets from one room to another; only in that world
could he find the seminal images that would focus his deepest
feelings into vision. And this process implies something about the
kind of meaning, and kind of glory, he would assume possible in
life; and remembering Podhoretz's remark that "lack of ideas is
no virtue in a novelist," we may say that, be that as it may, an

[7] The essay appeared in 1954.

idea any novelist has that does not come with some tang of experience, some earth yet clinging to the roots, or at least one drop of blood dripping from it, has no virtue for a novelist. Ideas without the mark of their experiential origin can only, to use Eliot's word, "violate" the consciousness of such a novelist as Faulkner. In *A Fable,* an idea "violated" the consciousness of Faulkner.

Podhoretz ends his essay by wondering "whether the time will ever come again when a writer will be able to dismiss politics in favor of the Large Considerations without sounding like a chill echo from a dead world." Again I must register agreement with the critic, not with his generalization but with the implication that Faulkner is an a-political writer. It is really strange that in his vast panorama of society in a state where politics is the blood, bone, sinew, and passion of life, and the most popular sport, Faulkner has almost entirely omitted, not only a treatment of the subject, but references to it. It is easy to be contemptuous of politics anywhere, and especially easy in Jackson, Mississippi, but it is not easy to close one's eyes to the cosmic comedy enacted in that State House; and it is not easy to understand how Faulkner, with his genius for the absurd, even the tearfully absurd, could have rejected this subject. Unless, as may well have been the case, contempt overcame the comic sense. Furthermore, in *A Fable* and *Intruder in the Dust,* novels that do impinge on political realities, Faulkner seems to have little grasp of them. In *A Fable* the failure is at root one of tone—we don't know how we are to take his fable in relation to the "realities." In *Intruder in the Dust,* Faulkner, like many other Southerners, black and white, including the present writer at one time in his life, may have been beguiled by the hope that the South, on its own responsibility, might learn to deal with the Negro in justice and humanity. The fact was that such a hope, in the face of the political realities (as a reflex, perhaps, from economic and certain other realities), and with the lack of courageous and clear-headed leadership, was a fond delusion. On this point, Faulkner was as much out of touch with the political nature of his own world as Camus was with the *colons* of Algeria when he tried to address them.

More significant than that hope was, however, the idea, expressed by Gavin Stevens, of a cultural homogeneity of Negro Southerners and white Southerners that would prevail against the rest of society. The whole idea is foggy in the extreme, and is foggily expressed, but, as I read it, it implies that the shared experience of the races in the South, for all the bitterness and tension, has created a basis for reconciliation. Some Negroes, in fact, have held this view—or hope—and many whites. But this bond, whatever its force or meaning, which is referred to by Gavin Stevens, came from a rural, individualistic society, or from a town life which still carried its values over from such a society. What Gavin Stevens (and Faulkner, and many other Southerners, white and black) did not do was to take a look at the Negro slums in the great Northern cities, and see there the shape of the future in the South as the mechanization of farming, and other factors, drove, and drew, the Negro from the land, and, in fact, subtly but deeply changed the nature of the whites who remained on the land. Furthermore, an "homogeneity" would, in the world of practical affairs, come too late to have any effect—certainly too late to seal off Mississippi from Freedom Riders, workers for CORE, SNCC, and SCLC, to prevent the founding of the Freedom Democratic Party, or to halt U.S. marshals at the border.

Gavin Stevens was talking some twenty years ago, and had not had the benefit of instruction from this morning's newspaper. It is easy for us, with the newspaper in hand and with the grass green, to say that we heard that grass growing. We can see things that Gavin could not, or would not, see, and among those things is one that has a certain comedy about it. In the South even in the small Mississippi towns like Philadelphia, McComb, Canton, Grenada, Greenwood, and Oxford, it will probably be the middle-class business men, the group for whom Faulkner cherished no particular fondness, and who, in Oxford, were not particularly enthusiastic about closing their stores and offices for his funeral, who, not from moral virtue or any theory of homogeneity, but from stark self-interest, once the message gets through to them that "nigger-trouble" is bad for business, will take the lead in working out some sort of reasonably decent racial settlement.

Faulkner was a-political, and he was, as Podhoretz puts it, "out of touch with contemporary experience"—if by contemporary experience we mean experience at the level Podhoretz specifies. But this leaves us with some troubling questions. For one, if Faulkner, because he is a-political, is not relevant for us, why do we still read such a-political works as *Moby Dick, The Scarlet Letter, Madame Bovary, A la récherche du temps perdu,* and *The Portrait of a Lady*—or an outright anti-political work like Shakespeare's *Troilus and Cressida?*[8] Or do we read them merely from academic interest, plus the incidental pleasure of being able

[8] A case might be made out that the politics of Shakespeare's History Plays and Roman plays is really nothing more than a façade, and that they, too, are basically anti-political.

to say that they are not "relevant"? There is indeed a problem of relevance, of what makes a work of literature specially valuable for one age and not for another. Works are not arranged in a great museum in a Platonic outer space drenched evenly by the chill white light of Eternity, bearing placards to indicate category and value. They do have a relation to the continuing life process, a relation of enormous complexity, certainly of greater complexity than is hinted at in the essay now under discussion. In fact, the whole argument for "relevance" as put in this essay has, as Podhoretz says of the work of Hemingway, Faulkner, and Dos Passos, taken on "that slightly stilted archaic look" of an old photograph—and the archaic look, in this case, is that of the 1930s, when it was fashionable to assert that a wide assortment of writers, including Flaubert, Proust, Frost, and T. S. Eliot,[9] were not "relevant." But those writers have, somehow, survived, and we even have the comic fact that Faulkner, who in those days was often rejected as the most irrelevant of all, was passionately read in places as different as Tokyo and Paris for the simple reason that he was taken to have something to say to the modern soul. The fact is that man, though a political animal, is many other kinds of animal, too. He is, even, a human animal.

I do not accept the basic thrust of the argument of Lewis, Kazin, O'Faolain, Podhoretz *et al.,* but I do think that these critics point to what might be called the defects of Faulkner's virtues, and I think that their views help to locate and limit some of the critical problems appropriate to Faulkner's work; for always when a reputation is resurrected from the dead—and some twenty years ago, in America at least, Faulkner seemed to be consigned to the shades—there tends to be, among the faithful as well as the newly redeemed, especially among the latter, the notion that the final revelation is at hand. Now, not only in the South but elsewhere, there is, clearly, the atmosphere of a cult about Faulkner, as there was about Eliot in the dark days of the Marxist dispensation, or about Pound in the period of rehabilitation.

Something of this tone appears in a letter by Russell Roth in *Faulkner Studies:*[10] "I have the feeling that many critics—most of them, in fact—would prefer not to see that what he [Faulkner]

---

[9] The game was carried so far that even a writer as definitely concerned with history and politics as Conrad, was said to be irrelevant; for instance, David Daiches, in *The Novel in the Modern World* said that Conrad was irrelevant because he was concerned only in the conflict of man against geography.

[10] Summer, 1952.

has been driving at. . . . What Faulkner says—is saying—cuts the feet out from under us; it flatly denies, or contradicts, or takes issue with most of our fundamental and most dearly cherished assumptions regarding our relation as individuals, to the world." There is, of course, always—no matter how often we may deny it—some issue of the kind and degree of "belief" in relation to any work of literature. True, there is more than one spirit and one way in which such an issue may be resolved—or it may be argued, with some plausibility, that such an issue can never be finally resolved, that in one way or another we must believe in a work or reject it. And certainly all really new work of literature comes into the world with the promise of a new view of man and the world, with, in short, a new doctrine, stated or implicit. The new work, even though it may seem to be merely a new style, succeeds only because of the promise, usually secret, of some kind of redemption.

There is indeed a value, though not necessarily the final or overriding value, in such a promise; certainly there is a value in the fact—or in what I take to be the fact—that the issues implicit in Faulkner's work are deeply central to our time. But a cult does more than recognize such situations and values. A cult really denies the complexities of such a situation. It equates, quite simply, the doctrine with the value of the work, or if sophisticated, finds the values of style, for example, an implicit affirmation of doctrine, the emphasis here not being on the inner coherence of the work but on the doctrine which the style, and other technical elements, may be said to affirm. In other words, the present cult tends to repeat, in reverse, the old error of the 1930s, to make doctrine equal value.

The long period of exegesis in Faulkner criticism has contributed to the atmosphere of a cult. Exegesis delivers meaning from the cloudiness of text, and there is only one step from this fact to the conviction that the cloudiness was an aura of mana, a sacred cloudiness, and that those who have penetrated it are saved and set apart. And it is well to recall that the snobbery of the cult merges with the snobbery of the academy, and that the process of exegesis has contributed to the sense that only by the application of academic method and in the exfoliation of theses can the truth be found, be packaged, and be delivered for consumption. The very classrooms—sometimes the very same professors—which once granted a grudging half-hour to document Faulkner's social irrelevance or perhaps his fascism, have now set about the canonization.

By and large, the cultism and the academic snobbery were accidental, merely an unfortunate by-product of a necessary endeavor. For the exegesis was necessary. Only by exegesis—such attempts at general schemes as those pioneering essays by O'Donnell and Cowley or such attempts at exploring the logic of method and style as the essays by Aiken and Beck, or the later studies of individual books—could the charge be rebutted that the work of Faulkner was, at center, pernicious or meaningless, and that the complications of method and style were no more than incompetence or self-indulgence.

But the period of exegesis seems to be drawing to a close. I do not mean that new exegeses will not appear. They should appear, if we are not to see criticism puddle and harden into an orthodoxy. But other kinds of interest are beginning to be felt, and will, no doubt, be felt more urgently. For instance, though much has been written about Faulkner and the South, much is repetitious, and there is clearly need for further thinking about the writer and his world. Related to this but not to be identified with it, are the questions of Faulkner's own psychology—his own stance of temperament. Both of these lines of interest are primarily genetic, they have to do with the question of how the work came to exist; but if this kind of criticism is pursued with imagination and tact, it can lead to a new awareness of the work itself, with a fuller understanding of the work as that unity of an art-object and a life-manifestation.

The most immediate need, however, is a criticism that will undertake to discriminate values and methods among the individual items of the canon. Faulkner was a fecund, various, and restless artist, and he paid a price for his peculiar qualities; some of the work is so uneven and unsure, so blurred or pretentious, that it provides apt texts for the most virulent of his detractors. We need a criticism that will do something by way of sorting out the various strands and manifestations of Faulkner's work, and by way of evaluating them. Furthermore, an overall definition and evaluation of the achievement has not been seriously attempted.

Undoubtedly, as in the natural history of all literary reputations, Faulkner's work will enter a period of eclipse. Though man is, not merely a "political" animal, but a "human" one too, emphases do indeed shift, with the shift of time, from one aspect of his humanity to another, and his tastes and needs change; what appeals to some of us now will not appeal to another generation. But it is the obligation of criticism not merely to assert the taste and needs of one age, but to try to discriminate what values, if

any, in a work may survive the merely accidental factors of taste
and needs. Criticism is, in part, committed to the task of trying
to build a bridge to the future. It is a hopeless task, certainly. It
is, even, superfluous. A work itself is the only bridge possible, and
that bridge may even lead the critic over into the future, where
posterity may gather around to regard him, perhaps, as something
as strange as the dodo or as blind as a fish drawn up from a stream
in a cave.

Part II The Major Novels

Frederick J. Hoffman

The Original Talent

I

Faulkner has several times referred to *The Sound and the Fury* as the favorite among his novels: ". . . I must judge it on the basis of that one which caused me the most grief and anguish, as the mother loves the child who became the thief or murderer more than the one who became the priest" (*Three Decades,**73). It was the most difficult of the novels to date, because the most ambitious. He tried to do several things in it: to narrate a continuous story, to experiment in forms of interior monologue, to represent four very different points of view with rich variety.

Faulkner described the experience of writing the novel, in his remarks to Jean Stein:

> I wrote it five separate times, trying to tell the story, to rid myself of the dream which would continue to anguish me until I did. . . . It began with a mental picture. I didn't realize at the time it was symbolical. The picture was of the muddy seat of a little girl's drawers in a pear tree, where she could see through a window where her grandmother's funeral was taking place. . . . I had already begun to tell the story through the eyes of the idiot child, since I felt that it would be more effective as told by someone capable only of knowing what happened, but not why. I saw that I had not told the story that time. I tried to tell it again, the same story through the eyes of another brother. That was still not it. I told it for the third time through the eyes of

*William Faulkner: Three Decades of Criticism, ed. by Frederick J. Hoffman and Olga W. Vickery (New York: Harcourt, Brace, 1963) [*ed. note*].

From William Faulkner *by Frederick J. Hoffman. New York: Twayne Publishers, 1961. Copyright © 1961 by Twayne Publishers, Inc.*

77

the third brother. That was still not it. I tried to gather the pieces together and fill in the gaps by making myself the spokesman. It was
still not complete, not until fifteen years after the book was published,
when I wrote as an appendix to another book the final effort to get
the story told and off my mind, so that I myself could have some peace
from it . . . (*Three Decades,* 73–74).[1]

These remarks at least suggest that the novel is constructed
upon a successive retelling of a single story from four different
points of view. The facts of the story are few and fairly easy
to record: the earliest significant event, the death of the grandmother in 1898, thirty years in the past; Caddy's affair with
Dalton Ames in 1909, the first of a series of affairs; her marriage to Herbert Head in April of 1910 and the subsequent birth
of her illegitimate child, Miss Quentin, which causes the annulment of the marriage; the suicide of Quentin, June of 1910; the
death of the father in 1913; and the elopement of Miss Quentin
with the contents of Jason's money box, and Jason's futile effort to
capture her, Easter Sunday of 1928.

These facts are told and retold four different times from
entirely different perspectives. In the first three cases, we are
within the minds of the three brothers—Benjy, Quentin, and
Jason, in that order—and adjust to their perspective upon the
story and upon the truth of it as each sees it. In Part Four, the
perspective shifts from an interior monologue to a straightforward narrative; the point of view is Faulkner's but the "inform-
ing genius" of the section is Dilsey. The effect of this arrangement,
once one has become used to it, is fascinating; and there is no
denying its appropriateness.

Robert Humphrey has made this shrewd observation about
both this novel and *As I Lay Dying:* Faulkner's "chief unifying
device . . . is a unity of action. . . . In other words, he uses a
substantial plot, the thing that is lacking in all other stream-of-
consciousness literature. . . . It is the thing that carries *As I
Lay Dying* and *The Sound and the Fury* away from the pure
stream-of-consciousness novel to a point where the traditional
novel and stream of consciousness are combined."[2] This is to say
that the usual stream-of-consciousness novel is concerned with

---

[1] When speaking of the "fifth time," Faulkner is referring to the appendix he
wrote of the Compson family history for Malcom Cowley's edition of the *Portable
Faulkner.* It was published in 1946, seventeen and not fifteen years after *The Sound
and the Fury.*

[2] *Stream of Consciousness* in *The Modern Novel* (University of California Press,
1954), p. 105.

revealing the inner minds of its characters, but that movement and action are only incidentally revealed.

The Sound and the Fury does two things: it plays upon the consciousness of Benjy, Quentin, and Jason, representing them in style, syntax, and image as nearly accurately as is consistent with the demands of the other task; it tells, and retells, a specific story, which has a sequence and succession of events leading through thirty years of Compson history. These two tasks are advanced in each section with an ingenuity and skill that enrich the account and give it a variety of meanings no traditional narrative could have achieved.

This novel is no *tour de force*. It is not what early critics accused it of being: a masterpiece of creative chicanery, designed to confuse and outrage the reader.[3] "By fixing the structure while leaving the central situation ambiguous," Mrs. Vickery writes, "Faulkner forces the reader to reconstruct the story and to apprehend its significance for himself. . . ." In this sense, the novel is a problem in definition, in the meaning or the "truth" of any human situation, as it is seen in very different ways. Mrs. Vickery also suggests in *Novels** (29) that the theme of *The Sound and the Fury* is "the relation between the act and man's apprehension of the act, between the event and the interpretation." Faulkner's characters are involved, many of them deeply involved, in trying to define an event to themselves. In this case at least, we are asked to become involved with them, since the only way the style will make sense to us is to have us look at events in the Compson family as each of the brothers sees them, in the act of their happening and in retrospect.

The central event of *The Sound and the Fury* is Candace's (Caddy's) affair with Dalton Ames. It is her "sin," her breach of ethics or contract, her act of bringing the outside world within the Compson family pattern. It is seen "out of proportion" in each of the first three sections; it is re-examined in part four and there seen as far less important than it had been earlier. Faulkner gives us both an inner and an outer view of it. He moves from one kind of subjective view to another, finally into the world itself, so that we may gaze at the place and the site of its happening. Truth would seem, therefore, to be a matter of perspective; we are aware not so much of truth itself but of a version of the truth, a distortion of it, which must be set right, and eventually is. Above all, Faulk-

[3] See *Three Decades,* pp. 16–17, for some contemporary reactions.
*Olga W. Vickery, *The Novels of William Faulkner: A Critical Interpretation* (Baton Rouge: Louisiana State University Press, 1959) [*ed. note*].

ner is saying that any truth is far more complex than it appears on the surface to be.

As we already know, Faulkner spoke in his interview with Mrs. Stein of "the picture . . . of the muddy seat of a little girl's drawers . . ." (*Three Decades,* 73). The incident occurs in 1898; Caddy, playing with her brothers in the "branch," falls into the mud and stains her drawers. In the evening Dilsey tries to rub out the stain, but doesn't succeed: "Just look at you," she says, "It done soaked clean through onto you." (*SF,** 93) The stain becomes the sin of her affairs, leading to Miss Quentin, the illegitimate child; and in the end the image of the mud stain is replaced "by the one of the fatherless and motherless girl climbing down the rainpipe to escape from the only home she had, where she had never been offered love or affection or understanding" (*Three Decades,* 73). The first three sections of the novel are concerned with the three distinct views of Caddy's "stain." Caddy means something different in each case; Mrs. Vickery has described it in *Novels* (30): "For Benjy she is the smell of trees; for Quentin, honor; and for Jason, money or at least the means of obtaining it." In part four, Caddy all but disappears, though her role in Jason's conflict with Miss Quentin is quite clearly in the background.

Faulkner adjusts the style, the imagery, and the narrative sequence of each of the sections to the point of view from which it is being written. Benjy's world is a fixed one, a world of sensations, one without time: all of these characteristics come from the fact that he is a thirty-three-year-old idiot who stopped growing mentally in 1898 at the age of three. He cannot abstract or generalize, cannot distinguish between one time and another, and can only react to a number of fixed sensory conditions that repeat themselves to him again and again. Here memory and sense are inseparable: a thirty-year difference in time is no difference at all, and sensations that are actually separated by twenty or thirty years are undifferentiated.

These characteristics explain the curious kind of fixed world we inhabit in section one; they also explain Benjy's instinctive reactions to any disturbance of that world. For example, Caddy when she is "right" to Benjy "smells like trees"; when she doesn't smell like trees, something has gone wrong; and Benjy sets up a howl of protest, his only way of registering a complaint or of passing a moral judgment. As in this case, when Caddy has been with

*Modern Library edition of *The Sound and the Fury* (1946) [*ed. note*].

"Charlie," one of a number of successors to Dalton Ames (the time is 1909):

> Caddy and I ran. We ran up the kitchen steps, onto the porch, and Caddy knelt down in the dark and held me. I could hear her and feel her chest. "I wont," she said. "I wont anymore, ever. Benjy. Benjy." Then she was crying, and I cried, and we held each other. "Hush," she said. "Hush. I wont anymore." So I hushed and Caddy got up and we went into the kitchen and turned the light on and Caddy took the kitchen soap and washed her mouth at the sink, hard. Caddy smelled like trees (*SF,* 67).

This detail is repeated many times, and Benjy's response to Caddy's departure from the Compson place in 1912 is sensed as a lack, an absence, which is compensated for by the sound of "caddy" on the neighboring golf course and by the presence of Miss Quentin, who becomes like her mother in many respects in Benjy's mind. The absolute limitations of Benjy's power to discriminate one thing from another, and one time from another, mean that we are in a fixed world outside of time and change. Benjy does not want change; it upsets him. He is quite incapable of seeing Caddy as a person who will change, grow old and exist in time. In a sense Benjy wants a simple world (the world more or less fixed for him when he was three) that does not change and is above and beyond the effects of passing time.

The strategy of placing Benjy's section at the beginning yields dividends: our first encounter with the Compson family is in terms of childhood (almost, of childlike innocence); it is a simple world, from which all decline and decay and breakdown are to begin. As we encounter family events later in the novel, we do so with the memory of Benjy's original and "pure" response to them. Finally, Benjy's non-abstract, overly simple "moral sense" is reduced to a number of minimal responses: he senses, smells evil, and passes an instinctive judgment upon elementary disruptions of a fixed world.

The Benjy section closes with a series of quick alternations of farthest past and immediate present—the present of Easter Saturday, April 7, 1928, Benjy's birthday. As Benjy undresses in 1928, he watches Miss Quentin escape down the pear tree outside their rooms (the two trees, of 1898 and 1928, fuse, as do the two persons): ". . . We went to the window and looked out. It came out of Quentin's window and climbed across into the tree. We watched the tree shaking. The shaking went down the tree, then it came out and we watched it go away across the grass . . ." (*SF,* 92–93).[4]

For all its greater complexity, the second or Quentin's section also presents a fixed world which he is desperately trying to preserve—but for his own reasons. One notices immediately the difference of language, the variety of figures and allusions, the appeals to undergraduate erudition, the forms of "debate" going on in his mind along rhetorical lines. Yet Quentin sees Caddy in much the same way as Benjy: in giving herself to Dalton Ames, she has violated a world that has before this been fixed; she has gone outside an established place and time, has set time and growth and decay going. Quentin also protests, in his own way, as violently and as vigorously as Benjy.

In his appendix to the *Portable Faulkner* (the "fifth attempt" to write the story), Faulkner speaks of Quentin as the person "who loved not his sister's body but some concept of Compson honor precariously and (he knew well) supported by the minute fragile membrane of her maidenhead as a miniature replica as all the whole vast globy earth may be poised on the nose of a trained seal . . ." (*SF,* 9). Quentin's mission is to save the Compson "honor" by arresting time and thus forcing decay out of the Compson world. He is in love with stasis, represented variously by the *place* of the Compson home, by Caddy's virginity, and eventually by death itself.

Quentin's great and powerful enemy is time—clock and calendar time—and he fights it throughout his day of June 2, 1910. Mrs. Vickery describes his world in *Novels* (37) as "an ethical order based on words, on 'fine, dead sounds,' the meaning of which he has yet to learn. He has, in short, separated ethics from the total context of humanity." In his own way, Faulkner has made this difference between words and humanity one of his major themes throughout his work. Similarly, Quentin demands that Caddy remain "outside of time," but she is in time and cannot break from it; she is a time creature and will therefore of necessity violate both Benjy's percept and Quentin's concept of a fixed world.

[4] The original is in italics, and generally speaking Faulkner intended italics to indicate a shift from one time fragment to another. See Lawrence Bowling, *Kenyon Review,* 10 (Autumn, 1948), 552–66, for a study of this and other matters of Faulkner's technique (also in *William Faulkner: Two Decades of Criticism,* Michigan State University Press, 1951, pp. 165–79). Note that Faulkner, in his remarks to Mrs. Stein, replaces the pear tree with a rainpipe, as Miss Quentin's means of escape.

Quentin sets himself the role of guardian of the Compson honor. Within the design of what he assumes it to be, he tries to set up his own system of rewards and punishments, of good and evil. Quentin is aware, on this day at Harvard, of the relentless move of time from light to darkness, from his life to his death. Clocks and watches tell the time, and he desperately tries to prove them wrong or unreliable. His body casts a shadow, as does his life as it moves within the years of family history; he tries to stamp out the shadow, and eventually succeeds with his suicide. But the shadow is just one of the reminders of the natural order: the odor of the honeysuckle takes him back to Mississippi, to Caddy's wedding to Herbert Head, and to the unavoidable facts of time and change. The honeysuckle is a sexual reminder, a reminder of rank luxuriant growth and decay, signalized in Caddy's illicit affairs. When the "paradise" of his childhood world fails, he tries to convert Caddy's sin into incest, to contain it within a fixed world he can control. He will change a paradise into hell, so that it be his own: *"Only you and me then amid the pointing and the horror walled by the clean flame"*[5] (*SF,* 136). As George M. O'Donnell has said, he is trying to "transform meaningless degeneracy into significant doom" (*Three Decades,* 86).

Quentin's efforts are not merely causeless quixoticism. His monologue reveals again and again the failure of the Compson family to hold together. This passage, for example, from his memory of Caddy's wedding in April, 1910 suggests a number of themes that converge upon Quentin's final act:

> There was no nigger in this street car, and the hats unbleached as yet flowing past under the window. Going to Harvard. [the street car, but also Quentin of a year before] We have sold Benjy's [the pasture land sold by the Compsons to a golf club, to provide the money for Quentin's Harvard year] *He lay on the ground under the window, bellowing.* [Benjy, on the occasion of Caddy's wedding] *we have sold Benjy's pasture so that Quentin may go to Harvard* a brother to you. Your little brother.

These last phrases are spoken by Mrs. Compson, and the time shift from the June day at Harvard to April of 1909 has been achieved.

You should have a car [Herbert Head speaking] it's done you no end

---

[5] That is, it will be a hell of their choosing, in which they are fully aware of their crime, like the position of Paolo and Francesca of Dante's *Inferno.*

of good dont you think so Quentin I call him Quentin at once you see
I have heard so much about him from Candace.

In the paragraph following, Mrs. Compson's remarks bring on
a flow of tortured memory, of Quentin's attempts to wipe out Caddy's sin by claiming it as incest, and it ends with a complaint of
his mother's total inadequacy:

Why shouldn't you I want my boys to be more than friends yes Candace and Quentin more than friends *Father I have committed* [Quen-
tin to his father, but an echo of the prayer of confession, showing
Quentin's appropriation of religion to his own moral world] what a
pity you had no brother or sister [his mother, to Herbert Head] *No
sister no sister had no sister* Dont ask Quentin he and Mr. Compson
both feel a little insulted when I am strong enough to come down to
the table I am going on nerve I'll pay for it after it's all over and you
have taken my little daughter away from me *My little sister had no.
If I could say Mother. Mother* (*SF*, 113–14).

Quentin's section concludes with a brilliantly represented
debate with the memory of his father's words. As he prepares to
go to his suicide by drowning (for which he has been preparing
throughout the day), echoes haunt him of what his father has said
throughout his struggle against the knowledge of Caddy's sin. The
dignity of his act, as he sees it, is questioned by his father until
it, as well as Quentin's belief in it as an heroic sacrifice, is lost
altogether.

. . . and he we must stay awake and see evil done for a little while
its not always and i it doesn't have to be even that long for a man
of courage and he do you consider that courage and i yes sir dont
you and he every man is the arbiter of his own virtues whether or not
you consider it courageous is of more importance than the act itself
. . . you are still blind to what is in yourself to that part of general
truth the sequence of natural events and their causes which shadows
every mans brow even benjys you are not thinking about finitude you
are contemplating an apotheosis in which a temporary state of mind
will become symmetrical above the flesh and aware both of itself and
of the flesh . . . (195–96).

Jason's section, the third one, begins in a matter-of-fact "rational" way: "Once a bitch always a bitch, what I say" (198). In
the Compson family appendix, Faulkner calls him "the first sane
Compson since before Culloden and (a childless bachelor) hence
the last. Logical rational contained and even a philosopher in the

old stoic tradition: Thinking nothing whatever of God one way or another and simply considering the police and so fearing and respecting only the Negro woman [Dilsey] . . ." (16). This statement is of course an ironic tribute to Jason's reasonableness; it is like the "integrity" of Flem Snopes: limited, selfish, and inhumane.[6] To Jason, Caddy's sin simply means that because of it he has lost the bank job promised him by Herbert Head before the annulment of the marriage. He is out therefore to be recompensed for "breach of contract," withholds the checks sent by Caddy to support Miss Quentin, and saves the money in his locked tin box (which Miss Quentin rifles of its contents before she escapes).

These are the simple facts of Jason's consciousness. Without subtlety and rhetorical finish, it is racy and self-indulgent, bristling with spiteful innuendoes, withal "objective" and superficially graced with "common sense." Praised by his querulous mother as the only "sensible" Compson, he falls victim in the end to a kind of "legal illegal" irony, for in stealing his money Miss Quentin is not only getting her own back but also acting in the manner and spirit of Jason himself. So smart a man, as the Negro Job has said, can be outsmarted only by himself. Having cut off humanity, he is eventually defeated by it in the person of the "man with the red tie" (who is never otherwise specified) who runs off with Miss Quentin, and by a series of irrational disasters on his trip to recover his loot. Even to the end, however, he thinks of nothing but the "business deal" that has been revoked:

> . . . Of his niece he did not think at all, nor the arbitrary valuation of the money. Neither of them had had entity or individuality for him for ten years; together they merely symbolized the job in the bank of which he had been deprived before he ever got it (321).[7]

II

In section four we move, for the first time, into the world itself. We are still within the Compson family, but we are not involved within a Compson mind. We look quite dispassionately at

---

[6] On this question, Edwin Berry Burgum speaks of Jason's unpleasant character but is moved as well to admire him (*The Novel and the World's Dilemma,* New York, Oxford University Press, 1947): ". . . we begin to realize that behind this contemptible surface . . . is a savage obsession to patch the walls of Usher, at last without doubt crumbling. He and he alone of the entire family is making some attempt to restore what they were once proud of in the past . . ." (p. 209).

[7] This passage is from section four and is from Faulkner's own point of view: hence the third-person narration.

the house from the outside—as though we had crossed the street for an appraising look. In this perspective it looks diminished and not a little grotesque, and certain revisions of perspective (which we had suspected were due) now take place. The first is the move of Dilsey to center, as the only fully balanced and genuine personality of the novel. Faulkner associates her dignity and power of endurance with universal truths and values, which will become the final means of judging Compsons. In the remarkable opening paragraphs, Dilsey is shown emerging from her quarters, dressed in Easter "finery":

> The gown fell gauntly from her shoulders, across her fallen breasts, then tightened upon her paunch and fell again, ballooning a little above the nether garments which she would remove layer by layer as the spring accomplished and the warm days, in colour regal and moribund. She had been a big woman once but now her skeleton rose, draped loosely in unpadded skin that tightened again upon a paunch almost dropsical, as though muscle and tissue had been courage or fortitude which the days or the years had consumed until only the indomitable skeleton was left rising like a ruin or a landmark above the somnolent and impervious guts . . . (281–82).

We also become aware of what the others left in the Compson household look and sound like. Benjy looms before our eyes, "a big man who appeared to have been shaped of some substance whose particles would not or did not cohere to one another or to the frame which supported it . . ." (290). Jason and his mother appear together at the breakfast table, "the one cold and shrewd, with close-thatched hair curled into two stubborn locks, one on either side of his forehead like a bartender in caricature, and hazel eyes with black-ringed irises like marbles, the other cold and querulous, with perfectly white hair and eyes pouched and baffled and so dark as to appear to be all pupil or all iris" (295).

From these several objective portraits it becomes obvious that the one of Dilsey will dominate and that in its terms Faulkner intends a final perspective upon the Compson story. Mrs. Vickery says in *Novels* (47) that Dilsey represents "the ethical norm, the realizing and acting out of one's humanity; it is from this that the Compsons have deviated, each into his separate world. . . ." The perspective shifts not only to Dilsey but also to the Negro church, where the Easter Sunday services are to be heard. The major performer, the Reverend Shegog from Saint Louis, has a "wizened black face like a small, aged monkey" (309), but a powerful mission and message; it seemed that his body fed his voice to serve the mission. In his sermon about "the ricklickshun en de blood of de Lamb" (311), he turns to the simplicities of religious feeling, cutting through layers of Compson decay and reaching a universal level of judgment.

As Dilsey returns from the service, she mutters to herself: "I've seed de first en de last . . . I seed de beginnin, en now I sees de endin" (313). The beginning and the ending of the Compsons surely, since Jason will not contribute to another generation and Miss Quentin has fled from it. The house has collapsed, but its torture and its agony are finally put into a perspective not its own. *The Sound and the Fury* ends with the trip to the cemetery of Luster and Benjy. Luster mischievously turns the wrong corner; Jason, arriving just at the moment when Benjy bellows his protest against the derangement, violently sets the wagon straight; and it proceeds smoothly and serenely once more: "post and tree, window and doorway, and signboard, each in its ordered place" (336).

In the end, the novel is disposed of by the Negro servant and the idiot man. These serve to let us see the basic simplicities from which the Compson family has long since fled. We already know that Benjy's view is limited (he is a "Christ figure" only in a very limited sense[8]), that it has to be helped and ministered to constantly. This leaves us with Dilsey as "ethical norm." Nor should we take too seriously the suggestion that the Compson decline serves by analogy to represent the decline of Southern aristocracy.[9] The problems and responses within the novel are sufficient to the needs thereof. But, of course, they may lead to expansions beyond themselves—at whatever risk such expansions entail. Faulkner was himself to move outside and beyond the Compsons in *Absalom. . . .*

[8] Several critics have made much of superficial parallels. One of the better considerations of this question is Sumner C. Powell's "William Faulkner Celebrates Easter, 1928," *Perspective,* 2 (Summer, 1949), 195–218. See also "Introduction," *Three Decades,* pp. 35–36.

[9] See Lawrence Bowling, *Two Decades,* p. 179: "The disorder, disintegration, and absence of perspective in the lives of the Compsons is intended to be symbolic and representative of a whole social order, or perhaps it would be better to say a whole social disorder."

Faulkner on

The Sound and the Fury

. . . Q. Mr. Faulkner, in *The Sound and the Fury* the first three sections of that book are narrated by one of the four Compson children, and in view of the fact that Caddy figures so prominently, is there any particular reason why you didn't have a section with —giving her views or impressions of what went on?

A. That's a good question. That—the explanation of that whole book is in that. It began with the picture of the little girl's muddy drawers, climbing that tree to look in the parlor window with her brothers that didn't have the courage to climb the tree waiting to see what she saw. And I tried first to tell it with one brother, and that wasn't enough. That was Section One. I tried with another brother, and that wasn't enough. That was Section Two. I tried the third brother, because Caddy was still to me too beautiful and too moving to reduce her to telling what was going on, that it would be more passionate to see her through some-body else's eyes, I thought. And that failed and I tried myself—the fourth section—to tell what happened, and I still failed.

. . .

Q. Speaking of Caddy, is there any way of getting her back from the clutches of the Nazis, where she ends up in the Appendix?

A. I think that that would be a betrayal of Caddy, that it is best to leave her where she is. If she were resurrected there'd be something a little shabby, a little ani-climactic about it, about this. Her tragedy to me is the best I could do with it—unless, as I said, I could start over and write the book again and that can't be.

. . .

Reprinted with permission by the University of Virginia Press, copyright 1959. From Faulkner in the University: Class Conferences at the University of Virginia, 1957–58, *Frederick L. Gwynn and Joseph L. Blotner, eds., Vintage Books.*

Q. Mr. Faulkner, I am interested in the symbolism in *The Sound and the Fury,* and I wasn't able to figure exactly the significance of the shadow symbol in Quentin. It's referred to over and over again: he steps in the shadow, shadow is before him, the shadow is often after him. Well then, what is the significance of this shadow?

A. That wasn't a deliberate symbolism. I would say that that shadow that stayed on his mind so much was foreknowledge of his own death, that he was—Death is here, shall I step into it, or shall I step away from it a little longer? I won't escape it, but shall I accept it now or shall I put it off until next Friday? I think that if it had any reason that must have been it.

. . .

Q. You had said previously that *The Sound and the Fury* came from the impression of a little girl up in a tree, and I wondered how you built it from that, and whether you just, as you said, let the story develop itself?

A. Well, impression is the wrong word. It's more an image, a very moving image to me was of the children. 'Course, we didn't know at that time that one was an idiot, but they were three boys, one was a girl and the girl was the only one that was brave enough to climb that tree to look in the forbidden window to see what was going on. And that's what the book—and it took the rest of the four hundred pages to explain why she was brave enough to climb the tree to look in the window. It was an image, a picture to me, a very moving one, which was symbolized by the muddy bottom of her drawers as her brothers looked up into the apple tree that she had climbed to look in the window. And the symbolism of the muddy bottom of the drawers became the lost Caddy, which had caused one brother to commit suicide and the other brother had misused her money that she'd send back to the child, the daughter. It was, I thought, a short story, something that could be done in about two pages, a thousand words I found out it couldn't.

. . .

Q. Mr. Faulkner, what do you consider your best book?

A. The one that failed the most tragically and the most splendidly. That was *The Sound and the Fury*—the one that I worked at the longest, the hardest, that was to me the most passionate and moving idea, and made the most splendid failure. That's the one that's my—I consider the best, not—well, best is the wrong word—that's the one that I love the most.

. . .

Q. Mr. Faulkner, in reference to *The Sound and the Fury* again is the "tale told by an idiot, full of sound and fury, signifying nothing" applicable to Benjy as is generally thought, or perhaps to Jason?

A. The title, of course, came from the first section, which was Benjy. I thought the story was told in Benjy's section, and the title came there. So it—in that sense it does apply to Benjy rather than to anybody else, though the more I had to work on the book, the more elastic the title became, until it covered the whole family.

. . .

Q. Mr. Faulkner, in *The Sound and the Fury,* can you tell me exactly why some of that is written in italics? What does that denote?

A. I had to use some method to indicate to the reader that this idiot had no sense of time. That what happened to him ten years ago was just yesterday. The way I wanted to do it was to use different colored inks, but that would have cost so much, the publisher couldn't undertake it.

Q. Doesn't that go on with Quentin, too?

A. Yes, because he was about half way between madness and sanity. It wasn't as much as in Benjy's part, because Quentin was only half way between Benjy and Jason. Jason didn't need italics because he was quite sane.

Q. And another thing I noticed, you don't advise that people have to have a subject and predicate for verbs and all those things.

A. Well, that—I think that's really not a fair question. I was trying to tell this story as it seemed to me that idiot child saw it. And that idiot child to me didn't know what a question, what an interrogation was. He didn't know too much about grammar, he spoke only through his senses.

Q. I'm referring mostly to Quentin and he certainly—he attended Harvard, he should have known.

A. Well, Quentin was an educated half-madman and so he dispensed with grammar. Because it was all clear to his half-mad brain and it seemed to him it would be clear to anybody else's brain, that what he saw was quite logical, quite clear.

Michael Millgate

As I Lay Dying

Several attempts have been made to establish specific relationships between *The Sound and the Fury* and *As I Lay Dying,*
to "pair" the two books,[1] and they do invite comparison as products of the same immensely creative period in Faulkner's career,
as two of his most ambitious stylistic experiments, and as his only
substantial adventures in "stream of consciousness" techniques.
It is arguable, too, that *As I Lay Dying* follows up *The Sound and
the Fury* in its treatment of a tightly-knit family situation revolving
upon a single female figure. Here the central figure is Addie, the
mother, instead of Caddy, the sister, and Faulkner seems to have
attempted to avoid repeating whatever inadequacies there may
have been in his presentation of Caddy, at least to the extent of
giving Addie one of the fifty-nine sections of interior monologue
into which the novel is divided. *As I Lay Dying* might also be said
to mark a development from *The Sound and the Fury* in that
Faulkner is now at pains to establish the setting and social context of the novel from the beginning:

> Jewel and I come up from the field, following the path in single
> file. Although I am fifteen feet ahead of him, anyone watching us
> from the cottonhouse can see Jewel's frayed and broken straw hat a
> full head above my own.
> The path runs straight as a plumb-line, worn smooth by feet and
> baked brick-hard by July, between the green rows of laid-by cotton,

[1] See especially Carvel Collins, "The Pairing of *The Sound and the Fury* and *As
As I Lay Dying* [*Princeton University Library Chronicle 18,* (Spring 1957)].

to the cottonhouse in the center of the field, where it turns and circles the cottonhouse at four soft right angles and goes on across the field again, worn so by feet in fading precision.

The cottonhouse is of rough logs, from between which the chinking has long fallen. Square, with a broken roof set at a single pitch, it leans in empty and shimmering dilapidation in the sunlight, a single broad window in two opposite walls giving onto the approaches of the path. When we reach it I turn and follow the path which circles the house. Jewel, fifteen feet behind me, looking straight ahead, steps in a single stride through the window. (p. 1)*

The geometrical and diagrammatic precision of this passage operates on a number of levels: as already suggested, the description carefully establishes scene and setting; but it also represents our first insight into the mind of Darl, creating that initial impression of absolute rationality and clarity of vision which is progressively dissolved as the book proceeds. It establishes, moreover, the basic terms of that conflict between Darl and Jewel which provides the major source of tension in this family novel, and which proves, in the end, to be the rock on which the family splits. The rigidity of Jewel is here opposed to the flexibility and circuitousness of Darl, and there is already a suggestion of the contrast between Jewel's fierce masculinity and that femininity of Darl's which is associated with his powers of intuition and which thus provokes the anger and enmity of Dewey Dell.[2]

The associated drama of Darl's personal breakdown recalls that of Quentin Compson in *The Sound and the Fury,* and Darl's vision, his perception of the world and of himself, undoubtedly has something in common with Quentin's state of mind on the day of his suicide:

In a strange room you must empty yourself for sleep. And before you are emptied for sleep, what are you. And when you are emptied for sleep, you are not. And when you are filled with sleep, you never were. I dont know what I am. I dont know if I am or not. Jewel knows he is, because he does not know that he does not know whether he is or not. He cannot empty himself for sleep because he is not what he is and he is what he is not. Beyond the unlamped wall I can hear the rain shaping the wagon that is ours, the load that is no longer theirs

*Page references are to the 1930 edition of *As I Lay Dying* published by Jonathan Cape and Harrison Smith [*ed. note*].

[2] I am indebted for this last point to Professor Meriwether, who also drew my attention to the important early essay by Valery Larbaud, "Un Roman de William Faulkner," in *Ce vice impuni, la lecture . . . domaine anglais* (Paris, 1936), pp.218–222.

that felled and sawed it nor yet theirs that bought it and which is not ours either, lie on our wagon though it does, since only the wind and the rain shape it only to Jewel and me, that are not asleep. And since sleep is is-not and rain and wind are *was,* it is not. Yet the wagon *is,* because when the wagon is *was,* Addie Bundren will not be. And Jewel *is,* so Addie Bundren must be. And then I must be, or I could not empty myself for sleep in a strange room. And so if I am not emptied yet, I am *is.*

How often have I lain beneath rain on a strange roof, thinking of home. (pp. 75–76)

This expression of Darl's uncertainty as to his personal identity— an uncertainty which leads eventually to a total disassociation of his personality and to madness—can appropriately be set against the central statement of Quentin's disordered perception:

I seemed to be lying neither asleep nor awake looking down a long corridor of grey halflight where all stable things had become shadowy paradoxical all I had done shadows all I had felt suffered taking visible form antic and perverse mocking without relevance inherent themselves with the denial of the significance they should have affirmed thinking I was I was not who was not was not who.

These passages also suggest certain thematic similarities between the two books. The idea of "twilight," for example, . . . is also important in *As I Lay Dying:* Addie Bundren is herself at the twilight point, the poised moment, between life and death; it is at the hour of twilight that she dies; and throughout the early part of the book the dying of the day and of the daylight is persistently linked with the moment of her death, somewhat in the manner of Shakespeare's Sonnet LXXIII.

More important, however, is the extent to which the whole journey to Jefferson with Addie's body becomes for Darl, and for the reader, an outrageous "denial of the significance [it] should have affirmed." We are challenged throughout the book, as throughout *The Sound and the Fury,* to confront and, so far as possible, to bridge the gulf that divides our personal systems of value from those adhered to by the characters; we are equally challenged to perceive and resolve the contradictions that necessarily follow from the use of multiple points of view. A major source of ironic, and often comic, effects in *As I Lay Dying* is the frequency with which characters are completely mistaken in their judgments of each other, and of themselves. We quickly realise, for example, that Cora Tull is utterly wrong about the kind and quality of the relationships within the Bundren family, while her own obsession with the cakes she has made prepares the way for the throw-away humour of Addie's brief but shattering reference to "Cora, who could never even cook." (p. 165) Of a similar order is the recurrent association of Jewel with images of rigidity—the description of him in Darl's opening section, quoted above, is reinforced by many subsequent allusions to his wooden face and eyes, his wooden back, and so on—in direct contrast to the inward passion and fury of his nature.

In *As I Lay Dying,* then, as in *The Sound and the Fury,* we are confronted with the problems of the elusiveness of truth, the subjectivity of what individuals call fact, and there is a sense in which these two novels together with the later *Absalom, Absalom!* can be regarded as a trilogy on this theme. In *Absalom, Absalom!,* as in the two earlier novels, the narrative is assembled from fragments; the central situation is progressively illuminated by the light thrown upon it from a number of different viewpoints, none of them possessing final authority. *As I Lay Dying* represents a development from *The Sound and the Fury* in that the authorial voice is entirely dispensed with, but *Absalom, Absalom!* goes a step further than *As I Lay Dying* in that we ultimately remain in doubt as to what has "really" happened, something which is not seriously at issue in *As I Lay Dying.* Here the concern with the many faces of truth merges with, and is eventually superseded by, the examination of the many meanings of experience—specifically, of the widely divergent purposes which the various members of the Bundren family hope to achieve in the course of their joint expedition to Jefferson. Regarded in this light, the multiplicity of viewpoints, which is much more marked than in *The Sound and the Fury* or *Absalom, Absalom!* and which may give an initial appearance of fragmentation, begins to appear rather as a means both of dramatising diversity and of focusing it upon a single course of action. A further focusing effect is achieved by the way in which the relationships within the Bundren family radiate about Addie, the mother, as both their physical and their symbolic core. Addie's powerful personality and the principle of family unity which she embodies have long held the family together and continue so to hold it at least until her body has been buried, and it is entirely natural that she should not only occupy the foreground of the novel throughout but become, in effect, the battlefield on which her husband and her children—especially Jewel and Darl—fight out their personal rivalries and antagonisms. What finally gives the technique its unifying force is the way in which the successive segments not only advance the action, the progress towards Jefferson, but continually cast light inwards upon the central situation, deepening our understanding of the characters and intensifying our awareness of their often violent interrelationships.

It has sometimes been suggested that the sheer profusion of points of view in *As I Lay Dying* is self-defeating, and there is perhaps a sense in which the *tour de force* draws attention to itself by its very brilliance. But Faulkner succeeds marvellously in catching the tone of voice of such characters as Anse—it is the skills evident in the Jason section of *The Sound and the Fury* which are being exploited here—and the use of a wide range of viewpoints gives moral as well as narrative perspective, offers scope for rich ironic effects, and broadens the sense of social reality. A clear distinction must be made, however, between viewpoints, such as those of Darl, Cash, and other members of the Bundren family, which display a developing internal drama, a progression from one segment to the next, and those, such as MacGowan's and Samson's, which are single expressions of an outside view. The technique of the novel represents, of course, a *tour de force* of conception as well as of execution, and in his determination to avoid any authorial intrusion Faulkner perhaps allowed a certain dilution of the tensions arising from the internal psychological dramas of his major characters. The centripetal effect of the technique might have proved still more powerfully cohesive if the segmentation had been less radical, if the points of view had been fewer, if they had been identified from the start, and if each one had recurred more frequently. On the other hand, the book as it stands offers a vivid evocation of the widening circle of impact of the Bundrens' adventure, an effect which harmonises with the circular and radiating techniques of the book as a whole and with its recurring images of the circle, from the circling buzzards to the wheels of the wagon itself.

It seems possible to speak freely of *As I Lay Dying* as a *tour de force* not only because of its obvious technical brilliance but because Faulkner himself often referred to it in those terms. He also said on more than one occasion that the book had been conceived in its totality before a word was written and that he had actually composed it in a period of six weeks.[3] These remarks have sometimes been misunderstood and are worth a brief examination. There is no doubt that the book was written very rapidly: the first page of the manuscript bears the date "25 October 1929"

[3] E.g., *Faulkner in the University* [Ed. Gwynn and Blotner, University of Virginia Press. 1959] p. 87.

and the last page the date "11 December 1929," while the carbon typescript is dated "January 12, 1930,"[4] indicating that Faulkner had not only written the book in less than seven weeks but had completed the typing up—usually, for Faulkner, a process of revision as well—in a further month. What does need some qualification is the suggestion that the book was written "without changing a word" and the further assumption, frequently made, that it went to the printer virtually unchanged. In fact, as George P. Garrett has shown,[5] the manuscript provides ample evidence of the way in which Faulkner reworked his material even as he wrote the manuscript itself, and further study of the manuscript reveals even more extensive revision at this stage in the writing of the book—for instance, in the Cash section on page 77 of the book. In the manuscript each of the separate sections is begun on a fresh page, and there is evidence that in at least once instance, that of the Darl section and the following Cash section, beginning respectively on pages 147 and 156 of the published book, Faulkner reversed the order of sections from what he had originally intended. There are also a few places where revised or additional material has been stuck on to the manuscript page: in the reproduction of the final manuscript page which appears as Plate V in the Faulkner number of the *Princeton University Library Chronicle,* the lines formed by the edges of two such passages can be faintly discerned. Faulkner made many more alterations and a few additions to the book at a later stage, presumably in the process of making the typescript, which is itself almost identical with the published book. The Vardaman section beginning on page 61 of the book and the Dewey Dell section beginning on page 110 are both considerably changed from the manuscript version, while the episode on pages 221–223 in which Jewel attempts to fight the man on the passing wagon who had commented on the smell from Addie's coffin is present in the manuscript only in rudimentary form.[6]

Clearly, Faulkner's remarks about the writing of *As I Lay Dying,* and of other books as well, are not always to be interpreted in a strictly literal manner. As he said to one of his last interviewers, speaking of interviews generally: "I'm liable to say anything on these occasions, and often contradict myself."[7] Writing

---

[4] *Literary Career* [by James B. Meriwether, Princeton University Library, 1961]. pp. 65–66. The manuscript and carbon typescript are in the Alderman Library [University of Virginia]; the typescript setting copy is at the University of Texas.

[5] Garrett, "Some Revisions in *As I Lay Dying,*" *Modern Language Notes,* LXXIII (June 1958), 414–417.

[6] Manuscript, Alderman Library, p. 94.

[7] Simon Claxton, "William Faulkner: an Interview," *The Cate Review,* June 1962, p. 6.

As I Lay Dying he said in 1955, was "easy, real easy. . . . I could write a book like that with both hands tied behind my back. It just came all of a piece with no work on my part."[8] Early in 1956, however, he mentioned *As I Lay Dying* in the context of a discussion about techniques:

> Sometimes technique charges in and takes command of the dream before the writer himself can get his hands on it. That is *tour de force* and the finished work is simply a matter of fitting bricks neatly together, since the writer knows probably every single word right to the end before he puts the first one down. This happened with *As I Lay Dying*. It was not easy. No honest work is. It was simple in that all the material was already at hand. It took me just about six weeks in the spare time from a twelve-hour-a-day job at manual labor.[9]

Faulkner wrote *As I Lay Dying* with unusual swiftness, writing at the very height of his powers; but he did not write it without effort, nor did he hesitate to make whatever subsequent alterations, additions, or deletions he thought desirable.

In both of the interviews just mentioned Faulkner went on to explain the essential simplicity of the conception underlying *As I Lay Dying*. "I just thought of all the natural catastrophes that could happen to a family and let them all happen," he said in 1955.[10] And in 1956: "I simply imagined a group of people and subjected them to the simple universal natural catastrophes, which are flood and fire, with a simple natural motive to give direction to their progress."[11] In essentials, it seems fair to say, *As I Lay Dying* is a simple anecdote recounted with a dazzling apparatus of techniques and in a manner that sometimes verges on the epic, resonant with biblical echoes of the Old Testament and of all the famous journeys of history, myth and legend: Odysseus, Jason, King Edward I and his dead Queen Eleanor. This aspect of the novel was early recognised by Valery Larbaud, one of those French critics to whom belongs the distinction of first taking the full measure of Faulkner's genius:

> Du reste nous pouvons, sans aucune intention de parodier le sujet de ce roman, le transposer en un épisode de caractère épique: l'épisode des Obsèques de la reine (homérique) Addie Bundren, conduites selon ses dernières volontés par son époux Anse et par

---

[8] Grenier, "The Art of Fiction", [*Accent* 16 (Summer 1956)], p. 172.

[9] *Writers at Work,* [ed. Malcolm Cowley, Viking Press, 1958], p. 129.

[10] Grenier, loc. cit.

[11] *Writers at Work,* p. 129; cf. *Faulkner in the University,* p. 87.

les princes leurs enfants: l'aîné, Cash, le très habile charpentier, boiteux comme Héphaïstos; Darl en qui un esprit de démence et de prophétie habite; Jewel, cru fils d'Anse, en réalité le "vivant mensonge", le fils adultérin d'Addie et du Devin (entendez le Reverend) Whitfield; et le dernier né, Vardaman, un enfant, et la princesse Dewey Dell, âgée de dix-sept ans, qui porte en ses flancs le fruit de ses amours clandestines avec un bel "étranger", Lafe, ouvrier venu de la ville pour aider à la récolte du coton (son prénom semblerait indiquer une origine scandinave: Leif?)[12]

What emerges even more clearly is that this simple story of poor farmers in the remote hill-country of northern Mississippi is deliberately presented as being played out against a background of cosmic scale. The atmosphere at the beginning of the book is repeatedly described as sulphurous and brooding:

> The sun, an hour above the horizon, is poised like a bloody egg upon a crest of thunderheads; the light has turned copper: in the eye portentous, in the nose sulphurous, smelling of lightning. (pp. 35–36)

When at last it begins to rain, "The first harsh, sparse, swift drops rush through the leaves and across the ground in a long sigh, as though of relief from intolerable suspense. They are big as buckshot, warm as though fired from a gun." (p. 71) Mood and setting are continually evoked on this grandiose scale, and there is a persistent invocation, in the description and in the imagery, of the elements of earth, air, fire and water: Addie, for example, declares that Jewel will save her "from the water and from the fire," (p. 159) while Dewey Dell compares herself to "a wet seed wild in the hot blind earth," (p. 60) and thinks of Darl's eyes as being "full of the land dug out of his skull and the holes filled with distance beyond the land." (p. 23)

There does not appear to be any consistent pattern designed to associate particular characters with particular elements: Faulkner's principal purpose seems rather to have been to enforce a reading of the novel, an interpretation of the Bundren family and its adventures, at a much higher and more universal level than either the characters or the action would seem at first sight to require or even to deserve. And, despite the outrageousness of the story, its frequent air of macabre fantasy, it gradually dawns upon us that this is in some sense a primitive fable of human endurance, an image of the tragi-comedy of all human experience. The family

[12] Larbaud, *Ce vice impuni,* p. 219. The final allusion is presumably to Leif Ericsson, Scandinavian Discoverer of America.

name, Bundren, even suggests a possible allusion to the burden which Bunyan's Christian carries with him on his journey to the Celestial City: Anse is specifically referred to as a man who has no burden but himself (p. 68), and he and his family can perhaps be regarded as making an ironic pilgrim's progress to the celestial city, the promised land, of Jefferson, where Anse at least receives his reward, in the shape of new teeth, a new wife, and a gramophone, while Darl discovers the path to Hell that leads even from the very gates of the celestial city.

With the brilliance of the writing and the immense centripetal force generated by the technique, *As I Lay Dying* is supremely all of a piece. Like *The Sound and the Fury,* it is written in a variety of styles, and certain passages seem over-written, or at least over-extended, as if the creative exuberance that informs the whole work had here overflowed into effects that were in excess of the needs of this particular book. Yet even in set-pieces such as the following, the distinguishing strength of the book is everywhere apparent:

> A-laying there, [says Anse] right up to my door, where every bad luck that comes and goes is bound to find it. I told Addie it wasnt any luck living on a road when it come by here, and she said, for the world like a woman, "Get up and move, then." But I told her it wasnt no luck in it, because the Lord put roads for travelling: why He laid them down flat on the earth. When He aims for something to be always a-moving, He makes it long ways, like a road or a horse or a wagon, but when He aims for something to stay put, He makes it up-and-down ways, like a tree or a man. And so He never aimed for folks to live on a road, because which gets there first, I says, the road or the house? Did you ever know Him to set a road down by a house? I says. No you never, I says, because it's always men cant rest till they gets the house set where everybody that passes in a wagon can spit in the doorway, keeping the folks restless and wanting to get up and go somewheres else when He aimed for them to stay put like a tree or a stand of corn. Because if He'd aimed for a man to be always a-moving and going somewheres else, wouldn't He a put him longways on his belly, like a snake? It stands to reason He would. (pp. 31–32)

Allen Tate recalls Faulkner telling him that this passage embodied the idea — apparently based upon a remembered anecdote — from which the whole book grew,[13] and it is tempting to think that the actual plot of the book, the story of the slow journeying with the decaying corpse, was also based on anecdotal material of this kind.

[13] Interview, September 3, 1963.

Its apparent predecessor among Faulkner's own works was the short story, "The Liar," first published in the New Orleans *Times-Picayune* on July 26, 1925. As Carvel Collins has pointed out, "The Liar" was Faulkner's first published story with a rural setting;[14] both "The Liar" and *As I Lay Dying* deal with the Mississippi hill-country and its people, both are concerned with the relationship between fiction and reality, and, as the manuscript of *As I Lay Dying* reveals, Faulkner at one time intended to use in the novel some of the same names for his characters as he had used in the story: Armstid's section beginning on page 175 was originally given to Stannes, while the MacCallum who appears on pages 102–103 was previously Mitchell.[15] When Faulkner said in the *Paris Review* interview that the speed with which he wrote *As I Lay Dying* was largely due to the fact that "all the material was already at hand,"[16] he may have meant, among other things, that he had been thinking about characters such as the Bundrens and their neighbours for many years, that he knew these people and their ways, and that he had a fund of anecdote and observation on which to draw.

In this, perhaps the most important, aspect of the book it seems fair to speak of Faulkner as having achieved something comparable to the Irish folk-dramas of Synge: there is much the same vigour of language, the same humorous realism, the same identification with a particular region and its way of life. Certainly Faulkner knew and admired *The Playboy of the Western World*,[17] and there is a passage in Synge's preface to that play which would apply with almost equal accuracy to *As I Lay Dying*. Synge has been paying tribute to the rich language of the Irish peasantry, and he continues:

> This matter, I think, is of importance, for in countries where the imagination of the people, and the language they use, is rich and living, it is possible for a writer to be rich and copious in his words, and at the same time to give the reality, which is the root of all poetry, in a comprehensive and natural form.[18]

[14] *New Orleans Sketches*, [ed. Carvel Collins, Grove Press, 1961], p. 26; cf. "The Pairing," p. 115.

[15] Manuscript, pp. 75, 45.

[16] *Writers at Work*, p. 129.

[17] "American Drama: Eugene O'Neill," *The Mississippian*, February 3, 1922, p. 5 *(Early Prose and Poetry*, p. 88) [ed. Carvel Collins, Little, Brown, 1962]; Faulkner here misquotes the speech of Christy Mahon, from the last act of *The Playboy*, in which occurs the phrase "mitred bishops," echoed in *The Hamlet, The Mansion*, and elsewhere.

[18] In John M. Synge, *Plays, Poems, and Prose* (London, 1964), p. 107.

A rich and copious language in combination with a natural and comprehensive presentation of reality: this seems a just summary of Faulkner's achievement in *As I Lay Dying,* and it is the multiplicity of stylistic variation as well as of viewpoint which is primarily responsible for the book's extraordinary success in holding in balanced and reconciled suspension its wide range of radically diverse elements.

Richard Chase

Light in August

There could hardly be a more characteristically American novel than *Light in August*—with its realism; its loose structure; its few characters who though vividly presented are never quite convincingly related to each other; its tendency to become a romance by taking on a legendary quality and by alternating violent melodramatic actions with comic interludes and scenes of pastoral idyl; its concern with the isolated self; its awareness of contradictions, racial and other; its symbolism of light and dark. Generally speaking, *Light in August* is in these respects akin to books apparently as diverse as *The Prairie, The House of the Seven Gables, Moby-Dick, The Grandissimes,* and *Huckleberry Finn,* not to mention *Uncle Tom's Cabin* and many others, including such novels of more recent vintage as Robert Penn Warren's *Night Rider* and Ralph Ellison's *The Invisible Man.*

In *Light in August* things are perceived in space rather than temporally as they are in *The Sound and the Fury.* Except for the Reverend Hightower, one of Faulkner's characters who are ruined by time, no one is particularly aware of time; and the surviving, enduring character, Lena Grove, lives in a timeless realm which seems to be at once eternity and the present moment. The Mississippi landscape spreads out before us and the faculty of vision becomes very important as we are shown the town of Jefferson, the houses of Hightower and Miss Burden, or the smoke on the horizon as Miss Burden's house burns. There is much use of the painter's art (even the sculptor's, as when Faulkner makes a wagon slowly passing through the countryside look like part of a frieze, or a seated person—Lena Grove or Hightower—resemble a statue). The art style is not cubist or otherwise modernist as it sometimes is in Faulkner's writing (*Pylon,* for example); it is serene, harmonious, and always aware, even in the midst of dark and violent actions, of a luminousness and spatial harmony that suggest an eternal order.

A simple and somewhat disconnected story emerges from the "abundance of representation," which, as Irving Howe correctly says, constitutes the splendor of *Light in August.* Lena Grove, a poor and ignorant farm girl from Alabama, painfully wends her way into northern Mississippi in pursuit of Lucas Burch, with whose child she is pregnant. Hearing that her ne'er-do-well lover has got a job at a sawmill near Jefferson, she goes there and finds Byron Bunch and Joe Christmas. But Burch has left; as the story goes on, Lena has her child and at the end is still on the road, an example apparently of perpetual motion. Now she is accompanied not by Burch but by Bunch; which one accompanies her she seems to regard as a matter of indifference.

Meanwhile in a long and exhaustive flash-back we are told the history of Joe Christmas, an orphan and (as everyone including himself assumes) part Negro. We are told how Christmas murders Miss Burden, a descendant of New England abolitionists, and how he is caught, escapes, and is finally murdered himself in the Reverend Hightower's kitchen by Percy Grimm. We are also told a good deal about the life of Hightower, particularly how he ruined his career and lost his wife because of his fantasy of identification with his Confederate grandfather, an officer in the army who had been killed in Jefferson during the Civil War. As the story unfolds, Hightower is now an old man isolated from the world, but before he dies he gets more or less involved with Lena and Joe Christmas and serves rather loosely as the unifying figure and center of intelligence of the last sections of the novel. There are thus three separate strands of narrative in *Light in August,* each having its central character. The book makes a kind of triptych.

Lena Grove is one of those intensely female females we meet in Faulkner's books, like Eula Varner in *The Hamlet.* A somewhat bovine earth mother, she has all those womanly qualities which, as Faulkner likes to point out, baffle, fascinate, outrage, and finally defeat men. According to Faulkner's gynecological demonology (it constitutes a sort of Mississippi Manichaeism) men are more interesting and valuable than women but the dark or Satanic principle of the universe decrees that they are the weaker sex and are doomed to be frustrated and ephemeral. Faulkner appears to agree both with folk superstition and Henry Adams that compared with women men are in Adams's word "epiphenomenal."

The bovine woman brings to Faulkner's mind echoes of ancient myth and ritual (hence the name, Lena Grove—cf. Hilma Tree in *The Octopus*) and he treats her alternately with gravity and with a measure of humorously grandiose fantasy and mockery. Lena's placidity is not only that of the cow but unmistakably that of the gods in their eternity. Hence Faulkner has given her a ritual office by associating her with the religious procession depicted in Keats's "Ode on a Grecian Urn," a favorite poem of Faulkner of which there are several echoes in *Light in August.* In Lena's unvarying inner harmony (and here Faulkner is serious rather than mocking) all opposites and disparates are reconciled or perhaps rendered meaningless. In the words of Keats's poem, beauty is truth and truth beauty. By implying that Lena Grove somehow symbolizes this ideal unity Faulkner suggests no metaphysical reconciliation. He merely praises again the quiet enduring stoicism and wisdom of the heart which he finds among the poor whites, Negroes, and other socially marginal types.

The first thing to be said about Joe Christmas is that he is not a villain, as is sometimes thought. Nor, except in a distantly symbolic way, is he a tragic hero or a "Christ-figure." He has many of the qualities Faulkner admires. He suffers, he is a divided man, he is marginal and bereaved; he is "outraged." He asks merely to live, to share the human experience, and to be an individual. Like the slave in "Red Leaves," he "runs well"—he has in other words some power of giving his doomed life meaning by insisting as long as he can on his right to be human. All this outbalances his being a criminal. It even outbalances his being a murderer.

It is the custom of some traditionalist critics to say, in the words of one of them, that "sentimentalists and sociologists are bound to regard Christmas solely as a victim," whereas actually he is a tragic figure akin to Oedipus. But the main difference between Joe Christmas and Oedipus (or any other tragic hero in the full classic sense) is that Christmas really *is* a victim; he never has a chance, and a chance, or at least the illusion of a chance, a tragic hero must have. It is true that in *The Sound and the Fury* and perhaps elsewhere Faulkner achieves a genuine tragic vision of life and evokes the profound and harmonious emotions that tragedy evokes. But on the whole his vision of things is more akin to that of "sentimentalists and sociologists" than to that of Sophocles—if by this we mean that, like many modern novelists, he takes a rather darkly naturalistic view of things but finds a saving grace in the simplest sentiments of men. Joe Christmas, as Faulkner presents him, is a character conceived not in the manner of the tragedian but of the naturalistic novelist. There is no mystery, no disastrous choice, no noble action, no tragic recognition. Instead there are heredity, environment, neurotic causation, social maladjustment. What happens later to Joe Christmas is made inevitable by the circumstances of his boyhood in the orphanage. In fact one may be very specific about the origin of the train of causes. Christmas's life is given its definitive bias by his encounter with the dietitian, described near the beginning of Chapter 6. Hiding in a closet and eating toothpaste, he has seen the dietitian making illicit love. When she discovers this, Christmas expects, and *desires,* to be whipped. Instead she offers him a silver dollar:

> He was waiting to get whipped and then be released. Her voice went on, urgent, tense, fast: "A whole dollar. See? How much you could buy. Some to eat every day for a week. And next month maybe I'll give you another one."
>
> He did not move or speak. He might have been carven, as a large toy: small, still, round headed and round eyed, in overalls. He was still with astonishment, shock, outrage.

What the boy wants is recognition, acceptance as a human being, if only through physical punishment. A whipping would establish the passionate, human contact. Instead he is given a silver dollar, and he sees his doom in its adamant, abstract, circular form. He has now been given an irresistible compulsion to destroy every human relationship that he gets involved in. And this compulsion includes the suicidal desire to destroy himself.

Joe Christmas thus joins the long procession of isolated, doomed heroes that begin to appear in the American novel with Brockden Brown, Hawthorne, and Melville. This is not the place to discuss the complex picture of Protestantism that emerges from *Light in August;* yet one may note that in the isolation of Christmas (and others in the book) Calvinism is still strongly felt as an influence, despite the fact that the psychology Faulkner has applied is generally "Freudian," in the popular behavioristic sense. Apparently nothing appears to our American novelists to be more terrible than to have become isolated or to have fallen victim to a cold, abstract hatred of life—nor, we must admit, does any doom call forth a more spontaneous admiration or require a more arduous repudiation.

But if Christmas has his American ancestors, Faulkner has

also made some attempt at modernizing him by making him in effect a Conradian or postromantic, existentialist hero. The portrait of Kurtz, the ultimately lost, rootless, and alienated man in Conrad's *Heart of Darkness,* is a distant model for Christmas. The Reverend Hightower, too, is a kind of Marlow (the narrator of Conrad's story), if only in the tone of his voice and in his physical appearance ("Hightower sits again in the attitude of an Eastern idol, between his parallel arms on the armrests of the chair"). And it is clear that Faulkner has learned some of his more florid rhetoric from Conrad. The following passage might have come from the pen of either Conrad or Faulkner; it is from *Heart of Darkness:*

> And in the hush that had fallen suddenly on the whole sorrowful land, the immense wilderness, the colossal body of the fecund and mysterious life seemed to look at her, pensive, as though it had been looking at the image of its own tenebrous and passionate soul.

This sort of thing has its own rhetorical magnificence, although both Conrad and Faulkner are perhaps a little too easily moved by the fecund, the pensive and the tenebrous. And there is no doubt that these authors—melodramatists both—tend to construct a rhetoric of doom and darkness in excess of what the occasion demands.

The Reverend Hightower is one of Faulkner's best characters. He appeals to us in many ways—first and most importantly in the sad everyday conditions of his life: the decaying house with the weather-beaten sign in front saying "Art Lessons Christmas Cards Photographs Developed"; the swivel chair in which he sits before the desk with the green shaded reading lamp as he gazes fixedly out the window; his moving colloquies with Byron Bunch, who, though his companion, is so different from him in heritage and intellect—as different as Sancho Panza is from Don Quixote (a parallel which is very much in Faulkner's mind). Only because Hightower is established in novelistic detail do we become interested in the fantastic obsession that has ruined his life. Like Quentin Compson and Horace Benbow (see *Sartoris* and *Sanctuary*), Hightower is one of Faulkner's intellectuals—he is fastidious, genteel, frightened by life. Haunted by the glory and crime of the past, he is incapable of living in the present. Like Quentin Compson he tries willfully to impose a kind of order on the irrational flow of time and nature. His view of things, however, is not metaphysical or theological like Quentin's; it is purely mythic and aesthetic, the product of a mind immersed in Keats and Tennyson.

A careful reading of the pages at the end of Chapter 20 will show that Hightower does not return to his earlier Christian belief in his moment of ultimate insight before he dies. The turn of his mind is to grasp truth aesthetically; truth is for him an ecstatic perception of a supreme moment in the natural, historical order, a moment in which, to employ the Keatsian vocabulary Faulkner encourages us to use, beauty is grasped as truth and truth as beauty. Before he dies he sees the truth about himself—"I have not been clay"—which is merely a way of admitting finally that neither truth nor beauty can be perceived by the mind that remains inverted and solipsistic and denies man's common fate in nature and time. This is the truth that finally comes to Hightower; and it is what allows him to see for the first time, and pathetically for the last, the full beauty of the myth he has lived by. For a moment he can now be free, for the first time and the last. The progression of his views has thus taken him beyond his Christianity and his pure aestheticism to a full, profound, perhaps tragic naturalism (to use the word in its philosophical rather than strictly novelistic reference).

A good deal has been written about the symbolism of *Light in August,* and although much of this criticism has been predictably beside the main points, it remains true that this novel has in it a much more complicated symbolism than *The Sound and the Fury* or *As I Lay Dying.* The most obviously conscious and willed symbolism is the least successful—such as the attributes of Christ Faulkner associates with Joe Christmas; these have an artificial, inorganic, even an arty quality about them. The symbolism that seems most profoundly organic with the action and meaning of the book is that of the circle, and I would judge that, like any interesting symbol, this was half consciously intended by the author but has implications within the book of which he was probably not entirely conscious when he wrote it.

Three circles should be kept in mind; they are associated with the three main characters. Remembering the theme of solitude vs. society, alienation vs. community that we noticed in *As I Lay Dying,* we remember also that Faulkner spoke of Addie Bundren's aloneness as a circle that had to be violated in order to be made whole. Although this is a literary idea that Faulkner might have absorbed from many sources, among them Yeats, the symbol of the circle of selfhood may be taken as an archetype of the modern imagination, and especially wherever Puritanism has made itself felt. Lena Grove's circle, then, since she is a kind of earth goddess, is simply that of the death and renewal of nature. She is also associated with the urn of Keats's ode and the ritual procession of its encircling frieze. In the circle of her being truth and beauty are perpetually absorbed into each other. In Lena selfhood is whole; it is congruous with experience, with nature and with time.

The circle associated with Joe Christmas is the fatalistic, repetitive pattern of his life; in actual symbolization it varies from the silver dollar the dietitian gives him to the pattern of his flight from the sheriff and his dogs. He wants, of course, to break out of his circle—"to define himself as human," in the words of Robert Penn Warren. Yet whenever this becomes possible, usually in relation to a woman he has become involved with, he succumbs to the irresistible compulsion to preserve his isolation. Finally, virtual suicide is the only solution. One might add that his circle is also racial; he is doomed to oscillate helplessly between the white world and the black.

If Christmas's imprisoning circle is imposed on him by circumstance, the Reverend Hightower's is imposed by himself, forged by his own intellect and neurotic fantasy. Only at the end when for a moment he is released from the isolation and stagnation of his life does the wheel that is a part of his obsessive fantasy finally spin free:

> The wheel whirls on. It is going fast and smooth now, because it is freed now of burden, of vehicle, axle, all. In the lambent suspension of August into which night is about to fully come, it seems to engender and surround itself with a faint glow like a halo. The halo is full of faces. The faces are not shaped with suffering, not shaped with anything: not horror, pain, not even reproach. They are peaceful, as though they have escaped into an apotheosis; his own is among them.

Despite the religious overtones of the language, this ultimate vision of Hightower seems to be a purely naturalistic intuition of his own solidarity with the other people he has known. It is this intuition that finally frees him.

The symbolism we have been noticing runs fairly deep, but it remains of the natural order, as, on the whole, does similar symbolism having to do with the self and its isolation in the writings of Hawthorne, Melville, and James. The specifically Christian symbolism in *Light in August* is not made deeply significant. It seems impossible to be much impressed with the fact that Faulkner calls one of his characters "Joe Christmas," and that he is thirty-three years old, has his feet votively bathed, and is in a manner crucified.

The symbolism of the circle would certainly, if we had here a specifically Christian novel, include the traditional symbolism of death and the newborn spirtual life. But this central mystery of Christianity is not present. And *Light in August* reminds us that Faulkner's imagination is not characteristically stirred by incarnation, catharsis, and harmony, but rather by separation, alienation, and contradiction. If *Light in August* were a Christian novel it might use the symbolism of the book as it stands—the circle, the opposition of light and dark, and so on. But in some way it would have to employ the idea that life comes about *through* death, that in some way a new spirtual life had come to the community of Jefferson through the death of Joe Christmas. But this does not happen; there is no new life, no transfiguration anywhere that would not have occurred without Joe Christmas. There is no new religious consciousness or knowledge. In Joe Christmas we do not celebrate the death and rebirth of the hero.

Light and dark, good and evil, life and death, Eros and Thanatos are postulated in *Light in August* as eternal and autonomous contradictions. There is no possibility of absorbing and reconciling these contradictions in a whole view of life that is in any specific sense religious, or, for that matter, tragic. There are only two courses open: (1) to commit some transcendent act of horror or violence or suicide, (2) to find reattachment to the simple concrete conditions of life, through love, stoic patience, or humor, for in this way one may, as it were, temporarily step aside from the eternal contradictions in which humanity is involved and give the world the appearance of harmony.

John Lewis Longley, Jr.

Thomas Sutpen: The Tragedy of Aspiration

In the beginning is the word.

In all the haunted, tragic world of Faulkner's imagination, there is no book so haunted as *Absalom, Absalom!* Either by instinct or design, he has made it, of all the novels and stories, the most epic, the most poetic, and the most essentially dramatic—dramatic because, more than any of the others, it is built on words and voices and nothing else. This is literally true. Both John Sartoris and Christmas are assigned a time and place in Yoknapatawpha; we hear them speak in their own persons. In *Absalom, Absalom!,* the beginning is curiously like a dramatic reading in which the actors come out in street clothes and sit at a plain table and begin to speak. Thus Sutpen exists only in the voices; he has his being only in reports of those who were told something by someone else.

In terms of pure form, this procedure equips Faulkner with a flexible medium that need not be anchored to any point in time or space. The way is therefore left clear for a complete freedom of development. The writer can make the hero, the story, and the narrators anything he wishes, since all of them can be defined only in terms of what the speakers remember, what they say, and the way in which they express reaction to events which exist now only in memory and must be reconstituted from memory. In the expression of their reaction and in the way in which they modify their reactions as discovery follows discovery, they too become emo-

From The Tragic Mask: A Study of Faulkner's Heroes *by John Lewis Longley, Jr., Chapel Hill: The University of North Carolina Press, 1963. Copyright © 1963 by The University of North Carolina Press.*

tionally involved and swept up into the pattern itself and reveal themselves as well. One by one, the author stage-manages the speakers forward: they each step inside the circle of the spotlight and say their piece. Each is like a spiritualist medium, evoking a ghost for his own purposes. At first Sutpen is one of a "barracks-full" of ghosts, undifferentiated and undefined, which the bored Quentin consents to be told about only for politeness' sake, a ghost who haunts Miss Rosa Coldfield's obsessed, impassioned voice ". . . as if it were the voice which he haunted where a more fortunate one would have had a house." Gradually, as the passion of what Miss Rosa is saying grows on Quentin, the ghost emerges:

> Out of the quiet thunderclap he would abrupt (man-horse-demon) upon a scene peaceful and decorous as a schoolprize water color, faint sulphur-reek still in hair clothes and beard, with grouped behind him his band of wild niggers like beasts half tamed to walk upright like men, in attitudes wild and reposed, and manacled among them the French architect with his air grim, haggard, and tatter-ran. Immobile, bearded and hand palm-lifted the horseman sat; behind him the wild blacks and the captive architect huddled quietly, carrying in bloodless paradox the shovels and picks and axes of peaceful conquest. Then in the long unamaze Quentin seemed to watch them overrun suddenly the hundred square miles of tranquil and astonished earth and drag house and formal gardens violently out of the soundless Nothing and clap them down like cards upon a table beneath the up-palm immobile and pontific, creating the Sutpen's Hundred, the *Be Sutpen's Hundred* like the oldentime *Be Light.*[1]

This is the classic technique of the empty stage—the two planks and a passion—out of which, as the various voices tell and retell what they know or must believe, the tragedy is born, a work that ranges over greater areas of meaning and extension than any other work in the Faulkner canon. But this freedom and extension of meaning is not obtained without a corresponding disadvantage. The work is "difficult," as any modern work is apt to be difficult, and the difficulty is compounded, deriving as it does from two simultaneous factors: the method and the meaning.

. . . In *The Unvanquished,* the form is simple chronological sequence, opening when Bayard is twelve and ending when he is twenty-four. In *Light in August,* Faulkner employs the technique of spiral form. With some oversimplification, spiral form can be

[1] William Faulkner, *Absalom, Absalom!* (New York: Random House, 1936), pp. 8–9.

defined as the technique of covering again and again the important point or cruxes of the work but always at higher and higher levels of understanding. Thus, early in the novel we learn that Joanna Burden was murdered and that Christmas was lynched for it. It is much later, only after a series of revelations and successive insights, that we learn the true nature of the relationship between them and the events that lead to her death. In *Absalom, Absalom!* the difficulty is greater in that, besides the necessity for gaining more information, the information when it does come is in the form of highly subjective personal reports, and we must learn how to evaluate them as we go along. But, as revelation succeeds revelation, the level of understanding progresses upward. *The Unvanquished* presents no problems to the reader and requires only a sympathetic response to be successful. In *Light in August*, the reader becomes more deeply involved as he identifies with Christmas' efforts to earn the right to his own self-definition. In *Absalom, Absalom!* there is a major problem. The reader must answer for himself the central question of Sutpen—what he really was, what emotions drove him, why he committed his seemingly inexplicable actions. From a third-hand, totally outside position, we must get inside the major protagonist. The method is invocation. The ghosts are invoked by a series of widely different mediums: Miss Rosa, frantic and eager; Mr. Compson, cynical, ironic, and mildly curious; Quentin, reluctant, then interested, and at last involved beyond recovery.

In *Light in August* the spiral employed by the author is cylindrical; that is, once the points or cruxes are established, the circle of reference moves upward but does not widen out. In *Absalom, Absalom!* the spiral is like an inverted cone, which with every recrossing or recounting of an event goes ever wider and wider into implication and expansion. In *The Unvanquished,* the essential action takes place within the community, the town of Jefferson. In *Light in August,* also, the important matter is the conflict between the community and Joe Christmas. In *Absalom, Absalom!,* the subject of the writer is cosmic; it is the law and structure of the universe itself that Sutpen is in conflict with. As Vincent Hopper has stated, Sutpen is "a satanic hero in the precise Miltonic sense that he dared to 'defy the omnipotent.'"[2] The sheer magnitude of Sutpen's grand design requires a matching magnitude of form and content: locale and time-span, geographi-

[2] Vincent F. Hopper, "Faulkner's Paradise Lost," *Virginia Quarterly Review,* XXIII (Summer, 1947), 415.

cal spread, and analysis of the meaning of history. The author has used several techniques for increasing the sense of a universal involvement. The events of the novel cover more than a century and range geographically far beyond the boundaries of Yoknapatawpha.

Here too, the technique of pulling in by statement and implication the matter of heroic, epic, and Biblical literature greatly widens and deepens the projection until the figures, particularly Sutpen, become larger than life-size. Tucked away in odd corners of the narrative are barrages of names, places, and incidents. Sutpen is a "widowed Agamemnon" and later "an ancient stiff-jointed Pyramus" and an "ancient varicose and despairing Faustus." His descendants of their various kinds are called "that fecundity of dragon's teeth." There are the obvious references in the names like Judith and Clytemnestra (that was a slip of the memory, says Mr. Compson; it should have been Cassandra). The real Clytemnestra is the vengeance-mad first wife, existing solely in the hope of some monstrous revenge for a monstrous affront to herself and her child. As in Greek literature and the Old Testament, the sign of evil is the violence it produces, which breaks out into dynastic fratricide or sets father against son and son against father. Charles Bon and Henry are like Absalom and Ammon, or an Eteocles and Polynices who love each other but are doomed by the grand design to kill each other. Of all the built-in implications, surely the most moving and most implicational is the title itself. Absalom was the beautiful but forever-lost son of David, a great king who founded an assured dynasty that would one day bring forth the Messiah. This, we will discover, is the compulsion that moves Sutpen: to get a son and found a dynasty. David had many sons to fill his lack, but Sutpen has only one that is acceptable to him. In the fullness ot time the Messiah is born, but the Sutpen dynasty ends with the half-witted Jim Bond—the end product of the sons Sutpen got. Thus Sutpen's mad design begins to assume the magnitude of a specific segment of history. Sutpen's failure springs from a defect of human feeling, the simple inability to feel and understand the feelings of others. Faulkner commentary has often rightly shown that Sutpen's racial attitudes are a part of his culture and that these same attitudes destroy the culture as well. What has not been shown is that Sutpen's dream of magnificence is typical of the United States as a whole, is indeed an example of the greatest American myth of all and thus is symptomatic of one national cultural failure.

II

In some ways, the discovery of what Sutpen was follows the classic pattern of thesis, antithesis, synthesis. The circumambient language winds through the spiral form, telling first one and then another version of what happened. In all the shifting points of view there are sudden, unsignaled shifts in time and shifts from narrator to narrator. There is an almost impenetrable pattern of relatedness and non-relatedness: those who were actually involved in the events were too involved to be objective; those who were capable of objectivity were too remote from the events. The novel begins at a very high pitch, with the near-hysterical, obsessed version of Miss Rosa Coldfield. Her thesis is that Sutpen was demonic, absolutely and damnably:

> He wasn't a gentleman. He wasn't even a gentleman. . . . fiend, blackguard and devil, in Virginia fighting, where the chances of the earth's being rid of him were the best anywhere under the sun, yet Ellen and I both knowing that he would return, that every man in our armies would have to fall before bullet or ball found him . . . a man who rode into town out of nowhere with a horse and two pistols and a herd of wild beasts that he had hunted down single handed because he was stronger in fear than even they were in whatever heathen place he had fled from. . . . And he was no younger son sent out from some old quiet country like Virginia or Carolina with the surplus negroes to take up new land, because anyone could look at those negroes of his and tell that they may have come (and probably did) from a much older country than Virginia or Carolina but it wasn't a quiet one.[3]

All this and many more pages like it are pure Gothic nonsense. The next account is that of Quentin's father: cool, rational, detached, unillusioned, or so it seems. If his account lacks Miss Rosa's passion and outrage, it also lacks power and conviction. We know Mr. Compson for a skeptic, but here he indulges in an almost contrary fault — speculation. His contribution adds little to that of Miss Rosa, simply repeating what is already known and underscoring Sutpen's character and personality. He comments on Sutpen's courtship, a process which Miss Rosa has insisted was a combination of sorcery and abduction: "They did not think of love in connection with Sutpen. They thought of ruthlessness rather than justice and of fear rather than respect, but not of pity or love. . . . it was in his face; that was where his power lay.

[3] Faulkner, *Absalom, Absalom!* pp. 14-17.

. . . that anyone could look at him and say, *Given the occasion and the need, this man can and will do anything.*"[4]

There is little in this to modify our view. After all, a summary of Sutpen's career is given twice in the first six pages of the novel. We have the story of his life in Yoknapatawpha, but there is no insight, no privileged glimpse into the wild and secret heart. Evidently, a totally new approach should be taken, perhaps at first hand. Such a narrator exists in Quentin's grandfather, Sutpen's only friend in Jefferson. Sutpen's trouble, says General Compson, was innocence. If demonism has no exact antithesis, perhaps innocence will do. In the Faulkner canon, the loss of innocence is usually followed by a predictable development, but Sutpen's history is exceptional. It is not that his innocence is crushed and destroyed but rather that he retains it in a distorted and misdirected form. Up to this point in the novel, Sutpen has been at a distinct remove from the reader; nothing reported of him is apt to generate sympathy. Here the author will do more than merely prepare for Sutpen's moral success or failure; he will make him human. With one stroke, Sutpen will be turned into the child we all once were — the child whose innocence and wish to be helpful are wounded by adult callousness in such a way that the child receives a mortal emotional injury from which it never recovers. Even at age twenty-five or thirty, Sutpen still does not quite understand the process himself. He has suddenly thrust upon him the thing he has to do. It is the last thing in the world he is prepared to do, but he must do it, if he is to live with himself and all the dead who have died to make him what he is and all the unborn yet to come.

Sutpen was born in the mountains of what would later become West Virginia. In the mountains there is a standard of excellence, however limited, which has nothing to do with property or possessions or money. A man is a man, and his manhood is measured by a tangible standard: whom he can whip, fair fight or stomp and gouge; what anvils he can lift; and how much whiskey he can hold. Possessions are few, and no one is so corrupt as to imagine that the ownership of things endows the owner with any particular virtue in the act of owning. But Sutpen, or rather his father, makes the mistake of coming down out of the Eden of the mountains (in which, roughhewn as it is, innocence is still possible) and in drifting backward into the Tidewater. Sutpen never knew that ". . . there was a country all divided and fixed and neat with a people living on it all divided and fixed and neat because of what color their skins happened to be and what they

[4] *Ibid.,* pp. 43, 46.

happened to own,—and where a certain few men . . . had the power of life and death and barter and sale over others. . . ."[5]

With the mountaineer's aplomb, he accepts things more or less as he finds them, becoming half-aware in the process of education, geography, race-conflict, and caste. The explosion does not come until the day his father sends him to the big house on an errand, and he is told by a monkey-nigger in a butler's uniform to go to the back door. He is little more than a child, but the mortal insult could not be clearer to him. Under the insolent stare of the house-servant, he feels the shame of his "patched overalls and no shoes." He goes away without haste or anger. It is not at all clear to him yet; he only feels the profundity of the insult. It is all foreign to his experience. He evolves the analogy of the rifle, the only terms in which he can explain to himself what has happened; the problem is to know what he should do. He momentarily considers killing the Negro or the plantation-owner, but discards the idea as meaningless. Realization comes all at once:

> . . . *There aint any good or harm either in the living world that I can do to him.* It was like that, he said, like an explosion—a bright glare that vanished and left nothing, no ashes nor refuse; just a limitless flat plain with the severe shape of his intact innocence rising from it like a monument. . . . this aint a question of rifles. So to combat them you have got to have what they have that made them do what the man did. You got to have land and niggers and a fine house to combat them with. You see?' and he said Yes.[6]

There follows the account of Sutpen in Haiti and his marriage to the daughter of a rich planter there. When he discovers that the wife can never be "adjunctive to the forwarding of the design," he returns her and most of the property to her father and goes to Mississippi. At the advanced age of twenty-five he must begin again. Cheating the Indians out of a hundred square miles of land, he drives his slaves and the French architect into dragging mansion and formal gardens out of the swamp. This done, he marries Ellen Coldfield. He is prospering; he has the biggest plantation in the county, a son and daughter. Now it is Sutpen who lies in the hammock under the arbor and has a faithful retainer to pour the whiskey. When Henry brings Bon home and Ellen announces Judith's engagement to him, Sutpen inexplicably forbids the marriage. War intervenes, and Sutpen apparently sets Henry to kill Bon. During Reconstruction, with Bon dead and

[5] *Ibid.,* p. 221.
[6] *Ibid.,* p. 238.

Henry gone forever, Sutpen seduces Milly Jones and then goads Wash Jones into killing him.

The manner of Sutpen's death, especially in the light of his lifetime effort to obtain his "better rifle" — the enormous plantation and the undoubted status that went with it — seems inexplicable. We are returned to a scene in General Compson's office just before the end of the war, in which Sutpen is quietly contemplating his past life, without anger or recrimination, with ". . . that innocence again, that innocence which believed that the ingredients of morality were like the ingredients of pie or cake and once you had measured them and balanced them and mixed them and put them into the oven it was all finished and nothing but pie or cake could come out."[7]

He explains the design he had, the acquiring of a plantation and a family, above all of a son to inherit it all and carry on the name. He reviews the circumstances of his first marriage: the birth of a son, the putting-away of that family, and the new start in Mississippi. From the perspective of what Quentin knows, it is seen that Charles Bon is the son of that first marriage. Shreve now believes Sutpen forbade the marriage because Bon was Judith's and Henry's half-brother and that Henry killed Bon to prevent an incestuous marriage. Now, after the war, both sons gone, all Sutpen has to do is begin for the third time to construct his dynasty. After Miss Rosa proves unwilling to test-breed, he begins the seduction of fifteen-year-old Milly Jones. When she is visibly with child, her grandfather, the pore-white Wash Jones, is still confident that Sutpen will "make it right." When the child is born, Sutpen tells the mother, "Well, Milly; too bad you're not a mare too. Then I could give you a decent stall in the stable." Wash cannot believe that the "Kernel" would treat himself and his family with such utter contempt; he kills Sutpen, the granddaughter, and the infant as well. Sutpen's arrogance and general demeanor show that he means to goad Wash into killing him, which seems incomprehensible in view of his repeated statement that all he wants is a son.

> *"Will you wait?"* Shreve said. "——that with the son he went to all that trouble to get lying right there behind him in the cabin, he would have to taunt the grandfather into killing first him and then the child too?"
> "——What?" Quentin said. "It wasn't a son. It was a girl."
> "Oh," Shreve said. . . .[8]

---

[7] *Ibid.*, p. 263.
[8] *Ibid.*, p. 292.

III

The wheel has come full circle. The little boy who was insulted and sent away has found his better rifle but in getting
it has succeeded only in killing himself with it. The circumstances
of the pattern are the same: the arrogance and intolerance have
produced a deadly insult to Wash Jones, a poor white who is a
child in everything except age. But here the insult is direct, man
to man; so the plantation-owner in the hammock must be killed to
wipe out the insult. The temptation to play on Sutpen's word
"design" is a strong one; the circumstances of the pattern are the
same. Perhaps the tragedy should end here. But the design Sutpen
has engendered is a tragedy of dynastic pattern, and the "fecundity of dragon's teeth" has yet to run its course. The insult to Milly
Jones is powerful and direct, and retaliation is equally quick. Still,
there is in the Sutpen design a rejection even more terrible and
more powerfully symbolic. Quentin and Shreve cannot put out
of their minds the image of Charles Bon, Sutpen's repudiated older
son—Shreve because he does not know and Quentin because
of what Clytie told him on that September night the year before,
when the House of Sutpen finally vanished in a holocaust of
flame, and what he has not been able to forget for a moment since.
Sutpen's forbidding the marriage is understandable enough; the
total rejection of a son so personally endowed, so genuinely more
aristocratic than the Sutpens is the mystery that must be solved.

The evidence thus far shows that Bon went to the Hundred
to meet his father at last, fully prepared not to demand any recognition at all, expecting the barest kind of private recognition and
acknowledgement, prepared to accept that and never cross Sutpen's door again. It is just this bare recognition, the simple words
"my son," that Sutpen cannot bring himself to give. When four
years of war have not solved the problem by killing any of them,
Bon feels his father has had long enough. He uses the only lever he
has to compel Sutpen to acknowledge him: he writes Judith telling
her to prepare for the wedding. Here Miss Rosa's hysterical in-
sistence on Sutpen's demonism seems almost plausible. All the
accidents of combat have not killed him; he has somehow intuited
the exact moment when Henry is ready to permit the marriage in
spite of incest. A demonic coincidence brings him to Henry,
whom he has not seen in four years. He tells Henry why the
marriage must not take place: Bon's mother had a tinge of Negro
blood. Even at this moment, he cannot bring himself to send any
word to Bon. As Bon makes clear, that one word, "son," even
now, would have been enough. Now he must punish Sutpen in

the only way he can, by riding with Henry the thousand miles back to the Hundred, so that Henry will have to shoot him dead at last. Now we know why.

IV

The rest of the story shows the working-out of the doomed House of Sutpen to the third and fourth generation. Bon has died to prove his right to be called a living human being. Charles Etienne St. Velery Bon seems to live only to fling his infinitesimal tinge of Negro blood in the face of Judith and the rest of the white community. We understand the hysterical response of Miss Rosa and Quentin and the others who have approached too near the maelstrom and could not avoid the knowledge from which they can never recover. Now the series of tableaux of minor person-ages surrounding the central figure of Sutpen begin to take on meaning. More than the single character Sutpen has come full circle; it is the tragedy itself. Perhaps, as Quentin says, any single act is like a stone dropped quietly into a still pool of water, and no one can ever know when the ripples stop moving. Late in life, Sutpen is described as an "ancient varicose and despairing Faustus." In exchange for the grand design of lands and an es-tablished dynasty, Sutpen trades his essential humanity—his soul. In some highly symbolic sense, Sutpen has signed a de-monic pact with his blood, if "blood" is seen as freighted with all its possible symbolic and ironic meanings: the blood of Milly and Wash, as well as that of all his children, black and white. The tragic pattern of Sutpen's career began in the innocence of primi-tive mountaineer virtue, received a mortal and undeserved insult, and resolved to match courage and strength, self-denial and per-sistence, in the struggle to wipe out that insult. In the tragic waste of such virtues, in the persistence at what ever cost, the tragedy is created. The price of the persistence is robbery, exploitation, and the violation of every human instinct including the withhold-ing of love in a blood relationship—which in the case of Charles Bon cost Sutpen his sons and in the case of Milly Jones cost him his life. Motivated by the insult dealt him in the arrogance of ownership and possessions, he lives his life only to die for inflict-ing the same insult. The old Oedipus who has been blind since birth still does not see the "mis calculation" of what he has done. All he wants is a son, and the son he is left with is the idiotic, saddle-colored Jim Bond.

As those acquainted with the greatest American tragic literature know, the sin of Sutpen is the unforgivable sin. In the terms of Hawthorne and Melville, he has not only isolated himself from all human commitments, he has committed the worse sin of violating the sanctity of the individual human heart; he has ruined not only himself but the lives and hearts of those around him. The list is infinite: he has abandoned his family in Virginia in leaving for Haiti; he has exploited the Indians, Yoknapatawpha, Ellen and her father; he has denied Bon, driven Henry to fratricide, and bent Judith to his ends; he has shattered the trust of Wash, seduced Milly and repudiated her and the child, driving Wash to triple murder; his legacy lives on in Velery Bon and Jim Bond. In view of all this, Miss Rosa's absurd Gothic demonism becomes sensible and Quentin's "Nevermore of peace. Nevermore of peace. Nevermore Nevermore Nevermore" is the only possible reaction to what has happened.

The impact on the present-day reader who is not involved, who can view the tragedy with detachment and aesthetic distance, is also explicable. What the reader is experiencing is *katharsis*. Aristotle was correct in stating that tragic events are most disturbing when they occur within the family or between close friends; this is only one factor that helps equate the Sutpen dynasty with older and more traditional tragic creations. All too often, the commentary on this novel has attempted to limit the frame of reference it is assigned to. Concentrating attention on the "race problem," the import is dismissed as terrible but as something local, Southern, and temporary. To be sure, Sutpen's sin is typical of his culture, and his downfall is symbolic of the downfall of that culture. The South is destroyed because it "erected its economic edifice not on the rock of stern morality but on the shifting sands of opportunism and moral brigandage." On a practical, realistic, American basis, the story is disturbing because we see in it a trope of one major American myth. Sutpen is only one more example of the kind of heroes America had before it created Horatio Alger, Jr. As everybody knows, in America the path to virtue and success is clear and simple, and any poor boy may follow it: marry advantageously, get a big house, and found a dynasty. The unspoken corollary is: get it at all costs, no matter how. When the boy Thomas Sutpen, ragged and barefoot, comes to the door of the plantation house, he is punished for the unforgivable American crime, the crime of poverty. This crime is unforgivable because poverty is the result of shiftlessness and well-known remedies exist for it. The remedy Sutpen attempts is the basis of his tragedy, which is cosmic in its import. As in *King Lear* or *Macbeth* or *Richard III*, the very frame of Nature has been wrenched awry, and blood cries out for blood.

"The South," Shreve said. "The South. Jesus. No wonder you folks all outlive yourselves by years and years and years. . . . except for one thing. . . . You've got one nigger left. One nigger Sutpen left. Of course you can't catch him and you don't even always see him and you never will be able to use him. But you've got him there still. You still hear him at night sometimes. Don't you?"

"Yes," Quentin said. . . .

". . . Now I want you to tell me just one thing more. Why do you hate the South?"

"I dont hate it," Quentin said, quickly, at once, immediately; "I dont hate it," he said. *I dont hate it* he thought, panting in the cold air, the iron New England dark; *I dont. I dont! I dont hate it! I dont hate it!*"[9]

[9] *Ibid.,* pp. 377–78.

Lawrance Thompson

The Hamlet

In the three novels which comprise the Snopes trilogy—
The Hamlet, The Town, and *The Mansion*—the subject matter
alone provides the most obvious factor of unification. Each of
the three novels deals with a different phase of predatory en-
croachments made by the Snopes clan. *The Hamlet* tells how they
achieved economic and social power in the little village or hamlet
called Frenchman's Bend, near Jefferson, early in the 1900's. *The
Town* tells how they swarmed in on Jefferson itself from 1905 to
1927. Finally, *The Mansion* tells how the most competent and the
most ruthless leader in the Snopes clan brought on himself a
mortal form of retribution, at the hands of a vengeful blood-
relative.

In each of those novels, the narrative mode is different. But
the distinguishing technical factor in *The Hamlet* is not the focus
of narration or style or structure; it is a curiously achieved tone.
That tone is initially achieved by Faulkner's capacity to laugh at
and to see something just plain funny in the grotesque and yet
thoroughly human members of the Snopes clan. Taken that way,
The Hamlet belongs with *The Reivers:* they are Faulkner's "funniest" books. Yet all the different elements of amusement in Faulkner's tone throughout *The Hamlet* serves a far more important
function. Underneath the laughter, underneath the comedy, there
is a very serious employment of comic and ironic elements for
satirical purposes.

As soon as a reader of *The Hamlet* begins to recognize the
ironic and satiric quality of the narrative, this account of Snopesism begins to acquire another kind of unification which is provided

From William Faulkner: An Introduction and Interpretation, *second edition, by Lawrance Thompson. Copyright © 1963, 1967 by Holt, Rinehart
and Winston, Inc. Reprinted by permission of Holt, Rinehart and Winston,
Inc.*

by the irony of one all-pervading theme which may be summarized as follows. Many of the evils attributed to Snopesism, and of course abhorred by all the characters who align themselves against Snopesism, happen to be evils which have been practised so long by so many of these other characters that they themselves afford unintentional aid and comfort to Snopesism. Although it may be granted that Faulkner's tone is only one of the technical factors which enables him to handle his narrative, here, with a fresh illusion of detachment and indifference, the unifying theme can scarcely be said to operate with particular subtlety. Nevertheless, too many readers have overlooked it, and too many critics have insisted that, ever since Faulkner created the first Snopes character in *Sartoris* (1929), he has used those two terms as allegorical types, to differentiate the goodies from the baddies. Such an egregious misreading, frequently praised and frequently quoted, was first formulated and published by George Marion O'Donnell in 1939, thus:

> In Mr. Faulkner's mythology there are two kinds of characters; they are Sartorises or Snopeses, whatever the family names may be. And in the spiritual geography of Mr. Faulkner's work there are two worlds: the Sartoris world and the Snopes world. In all of his successful books, he is exploring the two worlds in detail, dramatizing the inevitable conflict between them. It is a universal conflict. The Sartorises act traditionally, that is to say, they act always with an ethically responsible will. They represent vital morality, humanism. Being anti-traditional, the Snopeses do not recognize this point-of-view; acting only for self-interest, they acknowledge no ethical duty. Really, then, they are a-moral; they represent naturalism or animalism. And the Sartoris-Snopes conflict is fundamentally a struggle between humanism and naturalism.

That oversimplified parting of the sheep from the goats ignores Faulkner's persistently ironic unmasking of those Sartoris-like characters who, blind to their own inner elements of Snopesism, strike ridiculously pathetic postures of claiming that they detest and have nothing in common with Snopesism. That oversimplification also ignores Faulkner's treatment of the Snopes family itself, or at least of such members in it as Eck Snopes and his son Wall, who are represented as decent human beings struggling against other members of their own family. In short, that oversimplification ignores the continuous Faulknerian preoccupation with (to use Faulkner's own familiar words) "the problems of the human heart in conflict with itself."

One mistake of the Sartorises and their like, throughout the

Snopes trilogy, is their tendency to invoke ritualistic gestures of
the old tradition without realizing that their hollow formalism has
deprived traditional codes of whatever vital morality it once had.
To equate traditionalism absolutely with "an ethically responsible
will" is of course quaint. Faulkner satirizes precisely this concept
by letting certain characters like Flem Snopes imitate and adopt
some postures of "the old tradition" to provide a palpable veneer
of respectability. It should be noticed, however, that as the Snopeses start their climb up the caste-ridden social ladder, they do
not immediately come in contact with the typically Sartoris-like
characters. Throughout most of *The Hamlet,* Faulkner deliberately descends to low comedy; but in *The Town,* where the antago-
nists are led by the Sartoris-like Stevens family, self-deceived by
various forms of self-interest and yet ineffectually asserting their
desire to preserve the idealism of the old tradition, Faulkner finds
richer opportunities to blend compassionate satire with high and
low comedy.

Structurally, the four parts of *The Hamlet* would seem to comprise such an outrageous conglomerate of gossip, anecdotes, folklore, and tall tales that no pattern could possibly emerge. Part of
Faulkner's difficulty, in writing *The Hamlet,* must have been
caused by his choosing to perform a scissors-and-paste job, patch-
ing together pieces or wholes of six short stories which had previously existed as unrelated units, under the following titles: "Fool
About a Horse," "The Hound," "Spotted Horses," "Lizards in
Jamshyd's Courtyard," "Barn Burning," and "Afternoon of a Cow."
Although Faulkner revised heavily, and in some cases completely
rewrote parts of these stories, even changing to Snopes the names
of some non-Snopes characters, and relating them as "cousins,"
those revisions would seem to have been performed with a cavalier
laziness which did not entirely remove certain inconsistencies of
time, name, place, and distances, and certain unevenness in the
style. Nevertheless, one major structural configuration does
emerge from this conglomerate subject matter. At the beginning of the action. Flem Snopes, the shrewdest headman of his
tribe, moves in on the established order (such as it is) of the village called Frenchman's Bend, dominated by old Will Varner; at
the end of the action, Flem Snopes moves out of and beyond the
village toward more attractive goals of conquest, after he has ap-
propriated to his own uses all that he wanted out of Will Varner's
store, sawmill, and cotton gin and after he has even married Will
Varner's daughter Eula; in the middle, the action dramatizes the
hows and whys and wherefores of Flem's very successful depre-
dations.

Because *The Hamlet* is frequently referred to as "Faulkner's funniest book," it might be well to remember that Faulkner's kinship with Mark Twain, here quite clearly in evidence, frequently reveals itself with particular clarity in Faulkner's Twain-like combination of bland comedy and savage satire, the one on the surface and the other beneath. Like *Pudd'nhead Wilson, The Hamlet* is primarily a book of fools. In each there is no character who completely escapes from appearing decidedly foolish, at one time or another. In each, the author as narrator adopts a "dead pan" tone of detached indifference which merely heightens the homely wit and the devastating irony.

Because Faulkner does establish cumulative analogies between the actions of the Snopeses and the actions of their enemies, the reader needs to pay particular attention not so much to the obvious actions of the Snopeses as to the analogous actions of their enemies. The first chapter of the first book describes Frenchman's Bend in such a way as to make it vulnerable to precisely the kinds of amoralities which the Snopeses might count on using to gain an economic and social foothold. Without realizing it, Frenchman's Bend and the Varners had practiced Snopesism long before the first Snopes arrived. For example, after describing the original settlers, Faulkner continues:

> Their descendants still planted cotton in the bottom land and corn along the edge of the hills and in the secret covers in the hills made whiskey of the corn and sold what they did not drink. Federal officers went into the country and vanished. . . . County officers did not bother them at all save in the heel of election years. They supported their own churches and schools, they married and committed infrequent adulteries and more frequent homicides among themselves and were their own courts, judges and executioners. They were Protestants and Democrats and prolific; there was not one negro landowner in the entire section. Strange negroes would absolutely refuse to pass through it after dark.

The narrative tone there strikes the posture of amused unconcern, and the succeeding action is presented with the pretended detachment which is characteristic of Faulkner's comic method. The first description of old Will Varner preserves that tone of casual pleasantry, and thus subdues the ironic references to Varner as an upholder of law and order:

> Will Varner, the present owner of the Old Frenchman place, was the chief man of the country. He was the largest landholder and beat supervisor in one county and Justice of the Peace in the next and

election commissioner in both, and hence the fountainhead if not of law at least of advice and suggestion to a countryside which would have repudiated the term constituency if they had ever heard it, which came to him, not in the attitude of *What must I do* but *What do you think you would like for me to do if you was able to make me do it.* He was a farmer, a usurer, a veterinarian; Judge Benbow of Jefferson once said of him that a milder-mannered man never bled a mule or stuffed a ballot box. He owned most of the good land in the country and held mortgages on most of the rest.

The casual way in which that epithet, "usurer," is tucked between "farmer" and "veterinarian" keeps it from seeming to have any particular significance until the reader later learns that Flem Snopes also got his financial start in Frenchman's Bend by practicing Will Varner's kind of usury on Will Varner. For purposes of comedy, it is always pleasant to see two rascals posed as foils, each intent on punishing the other through shrewd horse-trading tactics. The reader can and does take a sardonic joy in watching both of them get hurt. Still other kinds of analogies between Will Varner and Flem Snopes soon accumulate. At the beginning of Book One, the first image clearly established is that of a forlorn and decaying Southern mansion, once owned by a prosperous planter remembered now as the Old Frenchman, whose abandoned treasures of money and silverware are still thought to lie buried in the weed-grown garden, now owned by Varner. Although the symbolic mansion is no longer fit to be lived in, its front lawn overlooks so many of Varner's business enterprises that he likes to sit there, in a crudely made chair which Flem Snopes will be occupying at the end of Book One. From that vantage point, even Varner can view certain kinds of people (himself excepted, of course) as fools:

> . . . His blacksmith had made the chair for him by sawing an empty flour barrel half through the middle and trimming out the sides and nailing a seat into it, and Varner would sit there chewing his tobacco or smoking his cob pipe, with a brusque word for passers cheerful enough but inviting no company, against his background of fallen baronial splendor. The people . . . all believed that he sat there planning his next mortgage foreclosure in private, since it was only to an itinerant sewing-machine agent named Ratliff—a man less than half his age—that he ever gave a reason: "I like to sit here. I'm trying to find out what it must have felt like to be the fool that would need all this . . . just to eat and sleep in."

Although V. K. Ratliff, the newsmongering sewing-machine agent who owns half of a restaurant in Jefferson, is certainly the

least foolish character in *The Hamlet,* his various shrewd attempts
to outsmart Flem Snopes eventually enable Flem to make a fool
out of Ratliff. Far more clownish in his ineffectual self-importance
is Jody Varner, the grown son and business partner of Will. Jody
"emanated a quality of invincible and inviolable bachelordom."
He set himself off from the overalls-clad citizenry of the village by
wearing, winter and summer and Sundays and weekdays, "a glazed
collarless white shirt fastened at the neck with a heavy gold collar-
button beneath a suit of good black broadcloth." That semire-
spectable garb is the one which Flem Snopes very soon tries to sur-
pass, after he has nibbled his way into the reluctant graces of the
Varners:

> . . . And the next morning he who had never been seen in the village
> between Saturday night and Monday morning appeared at the
> church, and those who saw him looked at him for an instant in in-
> credulous astonishment. In addition to the gray cloth cap and gray
> trousers, he wore not only a clean white shirt but a necktie—a tiny
> machine-made black bow which snapped together at the back
> with a metal fastener. . . . a tiny viciously depthless cryptically
> balanced splash like an enigmatic punctuation symbol against the ex-
> panse of white shirt which gave him Jody Varner's look of ceremonial
> heterodoxy raised to its tenth power. . . .

Fear, on the part of the Varners, gave the Snopeses their
first entree—fear, compounded by the futile attempts of Jody and
his father to outsmart and out-cheat the family they feared.
Flem's father Ab had ominously appeared at the Varner store one
day and had offered to rent an empty Varner farm on a share-
cropper basis. After stupid Jody had informally closed the deal he
picked up gossip that Ab Snopes had a bad reputation as a barn
burner. Before his slow wits could think up defenses, Jody found
out that Ab and his son Flem and two daughters and a wife and the
wife's sister had moved in. Thereafter, Jody countered his father's
warning to "stay clear of them folks" by insinuating his own plan
to out-cheat the cheaters: "Burning barns aint right. And a man
that's got habits that way will just have to suffer the disadvantages
of them." Within a week, as it happened, Jody was the one who
began to suffer the disadvantages: he found himself forced to take
out a precarious form of fire insurance through giving Flem a
clerkship in the store. Teasing Will Varner over Jody's moves,
Ratliff warns Varner that "there aint but two men I know can risk
fooling with them folks. And just one of them is named Varner
and his front name aint Jody." Modestly, Ratliff admits that it
"aint been proved yet neither" who the other man is. After his

first rough encounter with Flem, Ratliff sends word to Varner that "it aint been proved yet, neither."

As Flem expands his activities, he makes bad matters worse by calling in cousin after cousin to fill positions arranged for them. Each new Snopes is presented as being ridiculously picturesque in appearance or word or deed or name (I.O. Snopes, Mink, Byron, Vergil, Wallstreet Panic, Montgomery Ward, Launcelot Snopes, Vardaman Snopes, Bilbo Snopes, and even Colonel Sartoris Snopes). The thicker they come, the more outrageous the comedy, until Ratliff wryly imagines Jody Varner cornering Flem in the store long enough to say in a trembling voice,

> "I want to make one pure and simple demand of you and I want a pure and simple Yes and No for an answer: How many more is there? How much longer is this going on? Just what is it going to cost me to protect one goddam barn full of hay?"

So long as the Snopes problem discomforts only the Varners, the other villagers who have suffered from Varner's amorality can enjoy the huge joke. Only Ratliff is shrewd enough to worry, and unintentionally to prophesy his own fall, when he warns a few of the gossips that after Flem captures Varner's homestead "he will have to fall back on you folks." Flem has already begun such a falling back, and after hearing a few funny stories of Flem's usury, Ratliff gets indignant enough to start this conversation:

> "Aint none of you folks out there done nothing about it?" he said.
> "What could we do?" Tull said. "It aint right. But it aint none of our business."
> "I believe I would think of something if I lived there," Ratliff said.
> "Yes," Bookwright said. . . . "And wind up with one of them bow ties in place of your buckboard and team. You have room to wear it."
> "Sho now," Ratliff said. "Maybe you're right."

With that equivocal "Maybe," Ratliff restrains his indignation, although he does not agree with Tull and Bookwright. In spite of his limitations and his fondness for gossip, Ratliff seems to notice two different ways for taking the fact that whatever is nobody's business turns out to be everybody's business. If that ironic twist of words can provide one definition of mere gossip it can also be taken more seriously to serve here as a working definition of moral responsibility. Variations on the phrase, "it aint none of our business," occur and recur throughout the trilogy until that refrain accumulates extremely important thematic overtones. Ratliff, more than any other character in *The Hamlet,* resents and resists the moral dodgings implicit in that recurrent refrain. To that extent, he serves as a persona for Faulkner's own moral indignation. What keeps that usage unobtrusive is the fairly consistent narrative posture of Faulkner's seemingly amused indifference.

In Book Two, entitled "Eula," that same tone of indifference prevails as Faulkner describes the storms of passion which swept the village when Will Varner's luscious, lazy, cow-like, Junoesque daughter reached sixteen, got into sexual trouble, and had to be married off prudently. The first crisis with Eula had occurred when she was eight. Through some inexplicable irony her stupid brother Jody had become "erudition's champion" by insisting that Eula should go to school, even though the lethargic girl refused to walk the half mile and had to be transported to and from school by Jody. The next crisis was precipitated by Eula's decision, when she was thirteen that she had had enough of school. Her father's reaction was characteristic:

> "Let her stay at home then. . . . All we want anyway is to keep her out of trouble until she gets old enough to sleep with a man without getting me and him both arrested. Then you can marry her off. Maybe you can even find a husband that will keep Jody out of the poorhouse too."

In her fourteenth year, Eula increased her education when her clownish schoolteacher named Labove tried and failed to educate her in sexual matters. It did not matter to her father, "who seemed to have laid upon him already the curse of his own invincible conviction of the absolute unimportance of this or any other given moment or succession of them." In her sixteenth year, Eula had unintentionally aroused the marriageable young men of the village into a restrained frenzy, "a leashed turmoil of lust like so many lowering dogs after a scarce-fledged and apparently unawares bitch." Then warfare developed when an outlander named Hoake McCarron, who lived twelve miles away from the village, began to court Eula with considerable success, even though he had to fight off the combined force of his jealous competitors. Again her father's reaction deserves to be noticed because of its thematic importance:

> So when the word went quietly from house to house about the country that McCarron and the two others had vanished and that Eula Varner was in what everyone else but her, as it presently appeared, called trouble, the last to learn of it was the father—this man

who cheerfully and robustly and undeviatingly declined to accept any such theory as female chastity other than as a myth to hood-wink young husbands with, just as some men decline to believe in free tariff or the efficacy of prayer; who, as it was well known, had spent and was still spending no inconsiderable part of his time proving to himself his own contention, who at the present moment was engaged in a liaison with the middle-fortyish wife of one of his own tenants.

Mrs. Varner's reaction is equally revealing: ". . . Turning up pregnant and yelling and cursing here in the house when I am trying to take a nap!" Jody of course was different; he struck the "traditional" Sartoris posture when he protested to his parents, "Maybe you dont give a damn about your name, but I do. I got to hold my head up before folks even if you aint." (The Snopeses use precisely the same protest.) Jody's father tries to calm Jody by explaining the facts of life: "Hell and damnation, all this hullabaloo and uproar because one confounded running bitch finally foxed herself. What did you expect—that she would spend the rest of her life just running water through it?" To Will Varner, the situation merely calls for a practical move which he immediately begins to make. Bribed with money, and with a deed to the seemingly worthless Old Frenchman place, Flem Snopes finds ample profit in assuming the responsibilities of husband and father. He marries the girl and takes her off to Texas, for a honeymoon which lasts until after the baby is born. Ratliff, acquiring this gossip, is not surprised. It seems to him that Flem could outsmart the Devil and take over Hell itself.

Book Three, entitled "The Long Summer," interweaves three other ironically contrasted love stories; the loves of Mink Snopes, of Jack Houston, and of an idiot Snopes boy named Ike. It all begins with the ironically symbolic tableau of old Will Varner holding court in his store and serving as a Justice of the Peace to preserve law and order in an argument between Mink Snopes and Houston over the possession of a yearling bull—possession maintained by Houston during a full year without protest from Mink. When Ratliff hears that Varner has settled the case in favor of Snopes, he stands on the porch of the store sarcastically parroting the proverb-mixing gifts of the weasel-faced hypocrite schoolteacher named I. O. Snopes:

". . . Snopes can come and Snopes can go, but Will Varner looks like he is fixing to snopes forever. Or Varner will Snopes forever—take your pick. What is it the fellow says? off with the old and on with the new; the old job at the old stand, maybe a new fellow doing the jobbing but it's the same old stern getting reamed out." Bookwright was looking at him.

"If you would stand closer to the door, he could hear you a heap better," he said.

"Sholy," Ratliff said. "Big ears have little pitchers, the world beats a path to the rich man's hog-pen but it aint every family has a new lawyer, not to mention a prophet. Waste not want not, except that a full waist dont need no prophet to prophesy a profit and just whose." Now they were all watching him—the smooth, impenetrable face with something about the eyes and the lines beside the mouth which they could not read.

"Look here," Bookwright said. "What's the matter with you?"

"Why, nothing," Ratliff said. "What could be wrong with nothing nowhere nohow in this here best of all possible worlds?"

Ratliff, there serving once again as an equivocal persona for Faulkner, is interrupted by the appearance of the new store clerk, Launcelot (Lump) Snopes, who announces that the show is on and the men had better hurry: the idiot Ike is again making love to the cow in Mrs. Littlejohn's neighboring barn. The loungers and gossipers know that they can enjoy the peepshow from the rear of the barn. Throughout the long summer they continue to enjoy Ike until the day when they are interrupted by the voice of Ratliff, behind them, cursing. When one of them protests that even Ratliff has come to have his look, along with them, Ratliff replies, "Sholy. I aint cussing you folks. I'm cussing all of us." Then he lifts the plank and nails it back into place, concluding, "That's all. It's over. This here engagement is completed." When he tells Mrs. Littlejohn what he has done, she approves and strikes the injured posture of a Sartoris:

> "What do you think I think when I look out that window and watch them sneaking up along that fence?" she said.
> "Only all you done was think," he said.

As Ratliff goes on to rage against Snopesism, and to vent his suspicion that Lump Snopes must have had ulterior motives in letting this show continue without charging admission, Mrs. Littlejohn taunts him:

> "So that's it," she said "It aint that it is, that itches you. It's that somebody named Snopes, or that particular Snopes, is making something out of it and you dont know what it is. Or is it because folks come and watch? It's all right for it to be, but folks mustn't know it, see it."
> "Was," he said. "Because it's finished now. I aint never disputed

I'm a pharisee. . . . You dont need to tell me he aint got nothing else.
I know that. Or that besides, it aint any of my business. I know that
too, just as I know that the reason I aint going to leave him have what
he does have is simply because I am strong enough to keep him from
it. I am stronger than him. Not righter. Not any better, maybe. But
just stronger."

"How are you going to stop it?"

"I dont know. Maybe I even cant. Maybe I dont even want to.
Maybe all I want is just to have been righteouser, so I can tell myself
I done the right thing and my conscience is clear now and at least I
can go to sleep tonight."

Ratliff does stop it, even though I. O. Snopes protests with a
variation on the recurrent refrain: "If anything, Lump is going to
be put out considerable with what after all wasn't a whole heap of
your business." Without answering, Ratliff continues to make it
his business, thus further strengthening this very central facet of
theme. Faulkner invites the reader to differentiate, however, between the degree of accountability, or moral responsibility, which
might have been expected of the average citizenry, in their attitude toward the idiot Ike, and the contrasting degree of doom,
fate, victimization which predominantly controls the lives of the
three lovers juxtaposed in Book Three: Mink Snopes, Ike, and
Jack Houston. The tone of compassion which dominates Book
Three provides a striking contrast to the persistently sardonic
and satiric tone of the first two books. Pity is heightened by
means of flashbacks which implicitly illuminate the circumstances
that have shaped the predicament encompassing all three of
these characters.

The essential factor in Houston's story is his heritage of
ignorant fanaticism—a fanaticism which he never understands
even while all of his actions dramatize it. His marriage to a woman
he has known since childhood, a woman accidentally killed by a
horse six months after their marriage, was a marriage scarcely
leavened by love, or even passion, on either side. What bound
them in a compulsive attraction amounted to a kind of slavery
which neither one of them could comprehend. But her death
increased his harsh bitterness. Analogously, the story of Mink
Snopes's love and marriage is represented as another pattern
of compulsions, ignorance, and fanaticism. After he has settled
the altercation with Houston by killing him from ambush with a
shotgun, Mink returns home and notices his two young children
"looking at him with the same quality which he himself possessed:
not abject but just still, with an old tired wisdom, acceptance of
the immitigable discrepancy between will and capability due to

that handicap of physical size in which none of the three of them had had any choice. . . ." After describing how Mink's wife and children have left him and how his cousin Lump Snopes has pestered him with threats and pleas and cajoleries calculated to make Mink lead Lump to the dead man for the purpose of stealing whatever money they might find in his pockets, Faulkner could be referring to either cousin when he says that one of them possessed "an incorrigible dishonesty long since become pure reflex and probably now beyond his control." Thus the reader is invited to notice qualities, even in such Snopeses, which lie beyond immediate moral censure.

Faulkner's celebrated treatment of the idiot Isaac Snopes's love for Houston's cow constitutes an interesting change in stylistic pace. In this book of fools, the idiot Ike is an innocent, set apart from all the other fools, and not measurable in terms of moral codes. Yet, for these very reasons, which relate him to the idiot Benjamin Compson in *The Sound and the Fury,* Ike's actions can be interpreted poetically as providing a kind of moral mirror in which the actions of certain other characters are implicitly reflected and contrasted. As Ratliff tries to see what the men are watching through the aperture in the back of the barn, "it was as though it were himself inside the stall with the cow, himself looking out of the blasted tongueless face at the row of faces watching him who had been given wordless passions but not the specious words." All of Isaac's important motivations are provided by that "wordless passion." Even Houston, noticing how ingeniously Isaac provides food and comfort for the cow, is permitted to think "that there is perhaps something in passion too, as well as in poverty and innocence, which cares for its own." No expense of energy is too great for Isaac to make for the cow; he risks his life in saving her from the fire. His actions in tending her are selfless, his adoration makes him bring her flowers with the hay. Her presence, as she walks through the mist beside the creek in the early dawn, heightens all of Isaac's sensuous responses. He does not know what love is, and yet some of Ike's actions practically or figuratively dramatize certain meanings of love in a form far more pure and exalted than the actions of any other character in the book. So when Faulkner, in describing Isaac's love, permits his prose to ascend to a lyric intensity far greater than in any other passage in *The Hamlet,* that pastoral lyricism is not mere parody or mockery. If it mocks anything, it mocks the lack of love among the morally responsible characters. When Book Three concludes with the passage in which Eck Snopes explains to Ratliff why he has tried to provide compensation to Ike for the loss of his cow by giving the idiot a little wooden effigy, Eck's pity elevates him above all the other Snopes, and foreshadows certain actions in *The Town,* where Eck and his son turn against Snopesism, and fight it.

Book Four of *The Hamlet* returns to the comic and satiric mode while still intermingling elements of pathos, tragedy, compassion, and pity. The first section of it is devoted to the account of how Flem Snopes brought back from his Texas honeymoon a herd of wild spotted horses, along with a Texan who auctions them off to the countrypeople, and thus makes a handsome profit for Snopes, before the horses escape and run wild throughout and beyond Frenchman's Bend. The sheer narrative power of the account is obviously heightened by Faulkner's intense delight in, and knowledge of, horse flesh. The account of the runaway horse which invades Mrs. Littlejohn's hotel and nearly frightens Ratliff out of his skin is splendidly comic. Yet Faulkner successfully dares to combine pathos with comedy by permitting Henry Armstid and his wife to become involved in the auction. The plight of the Armstids helps to throw more light on the character of Flem Snopes.

When Armstid seeks revenge against Flem, the resulting action provides a fitting close for *The Hamlet. Money-money-money,* as a symbol of self-interest, has provided a recurrent motif throughout this conglomerate of narratives. Generally considered, a Snopes is anyone who will do anything, even sell his soul (if any), for money. Now suddenly Armstid and Bookwright and Ratliff are represented as having become sufficiently Snopesian to find themselves maddened by the conviction that there must be truth in all the old stories about money buried by the Old Frenchman in the garden back of the forlorn and decaying mansion. Henry has even seen Flem Snopes digging by starlight in that garden which now belongs to Flem. Perhaps as Ratliff suggests, he has found in the old house a map of the garden which has given him the approximate location of the treasure. If Snopes can dig until midnight, then his three money-crazed enemies can dig through the rest of the night. Ratliff enlists the help of an old man who is a magician with a diviner's rod and, during one exciting secret exploration, the old man helps them locate three small bags of money in the garden. That is all the evidence needed by these prospectors. At the end of that same day, Ratliff approaches Flem Snopes and finds him willing to sell the old Frenchman's place:

> A little after six that evening, in the empty and locked store, Ratliff gave a quit-claim deed to his half of the side-street lunch-

room in Jefferson. Armstid gave a mortgage on his farm. . . . Bookwright paid his third in cash.

Thereafter, they are free to dig in earnest. Fearing that someone will interrupt them, they dig only at night, and for three
nights they wear themselves out with frantic labors. Then it occurs
to Ratliff to examine the dates on the coins, and to his chargin
he finds that Flem Snopes has fooled them with the old trick of
"salting" an empty mine. A few days later, when the triumphant
Flem and his wife Eula pack their belongings into their mule
wagon and drive out of Frenchman's Bend toward Ratliff's restaurant in Jefferson, gossips notice that the road they are taking
will make the trip three miles longer than necessary. The wits
make guesses:

>   "Maybe he aims to take them three miles on into town with
> him and swap them to Aaron Rideout for the other half of that
> restaurant."
>   "Maybe he'll swap them to Ratliff and Bookwright and Henry
> Armstid for something else."
>   "He'll find Henry Armstid without having to go that far."

Henry is still digging at the Old Frenchman place, the gaunt
unshaven face "now completely that of a madman." Earlier, Ratliff
had said of Henry, without any boomerang intention, "Just look
at what even the money a man aint got yet will do to him."

Melvin Backman

"The Bear" and Go Down, Moses

The heart of *Go Down, Moses* (1942) is "The Bear." The most
widely acclaimed story of the seven in the volume, "The Bear"
has received a variety of interpretations. One critic has emphasized its New Testament spirit, others its romantic and transcendental character, and still others its primitivism and myth.[1] The
variety of critical response testifies to the story's density of
meaning. It is a rich, original story treating of a universal issue;
nevertheless, it is distinctly American. Lionel Trilling has placed
it in the romantic, transcendental tradition of Cooper, Thoreau,
and Melville, while Malcolm Cowley has associated it with the
work of Mark Twain. In its pastoral spirit "The Bear" does seem
related to *Huck Finn;* and, in its development of the wilderness

[1] See R. W. B. Lewis, "The Hero in the New World: William Faulkner's 'The
Bear,'" *Kenyon Review,* XIII (Autumn 1951), 641–660; Lionel Trilling, "The
McCaslins of Mississippi," *The Nation,* CLIV (30 May 1942), 632–633; Irving D.
Blum, "The Parallel Philosophy of Emerson's 'Nature' and Faulkner's 'The Bear,'"
Emerson Society Quarterly, No. 13 (4th Quart., 1958), 22–25; Malcolm Cowley,
"Go Down to Faulkner's Land," *The New Republic,* CVI (29 June 1942), 900;
Harry Modean Campbell and Ruel E. Foster, *William Faulkner: A Critical Apprais-
al* (Norman: Univ. of Oklahoma Press, 1951), pp. 146–158; Kenneth LaBudde,
"Cultural Primitivism in William Faulkner's 'The Bear,'" *American Quarterly,* II
(Winter 1950), 322–328; William Van O'Connor, "The Wilderness Theme in
Faulkner's 'The Bear,'" *Accent,* XIII (Winter 1953), 12–20; W. R. Moses, "Where
History Crosses Myth: Another Reading of 'The Bear,'" *Accent,* XIII (Winter
1953), 21–33; and Otis B. Wheeler, "Faulkner's Wilderness," *American Literature,*
XXXI (May 1959), 127–136; Herbert A. Perluck, "'The Heart's Driving Complex-
ity': An Unromantic Reading of Faulkner's 'The Bear,'" *Accent,* XX (Winter 1960),
23–46.

*Reprinted by permission of the Modern Language Association of America
from PMLA, LXXVI (December, 1961), pp. 595–600. Original title:
"The Wilderness and the Negro in Faulkner's 'The Bear.'" Copyright ©
1961 by Modern Language Association.*

theme, to Cooper's *Leatherstocking Tales.*[2] Yet because of the story's tendency to split into two parts—one part concerned with the wilderness, the other with the Negro—the structure of the story has seemed faulty and its meaning ambiguous. If "The Bear" is examined within the context of the other related stories of the *Go Down, Moses* volume, its meaning may be clarified.

The first story, "Was," is a warmly humorous introduction to some of the old McCaslins, white and black, before the Civil War. The next two stories, "The Fire and the Hearth" and "Pantaloon in Black," turn their focus upon the Negro. But the following three stories—"The Old People," "The Bear," and "Delta Autumn" —shift to Isaac McCaslin and the wilderness. The last story, "Go Down, Moses," returns to the Negro. The movement of the *Go Down, Moses* volume is from surface to depth, from comedy to tragedy, and from the ante-bellum past to the present about the beginning of the Second World War. The subject of *Go Down, Moses* is apparently the Negro or the wilderness, although in "The Bear" they are strangely merged. This merging of the Negro and the wilderness suggests that "The Bear" is not only the heart but also the climax of *Go Down, Moses,* since this collection of stories about the black and white descendants of the McCaslin clan of the last century is telling, in a sense, of the making of the conscience of Isaac McCaslin. It seems appropriate, therefore, to begin this study of "The Bear" with a discussion of the Negro, particularly as he emerges in "The Fire and the Hearth," and later, after a close consideration of "The Bear" itself, to conclude with Faulkner's final commentary on the wilderness and the Negro in "Delta Autumn" and "Go Down, Moses."

"The Fire and the Hearth" is concerned with two themes: (1) the Negro-white relationship and (2) family love. Its hero is the Negro, Lucas Beauchamp. Lucas was a proud Negro who had fought for his rights as a man. There was the time he went to fetch his wife from the white man's house where she had gone six months ago to deliver and nurse the white child, Roth Edmonds. Lucas confronted Zack Edmonds, his white kinsman and landlord: "'I'm a nigger. . . . But I'm a man too. I'm more than just a man. The same thing made my pappy that made your grandmaw. I'm going to take her back'" (p. 47).[3] She came back. But six months

---

[2] Ursula Brumm has commented on the relationship between Cooper and Faulkner, particularly in regard to the wilderness theme and the affinity between Sam Fathers and Natty Bumpo. See Ursula Brumm, "Wilderness and Civilization: A Note on William Faulkner," *Partisan Review,* XXII (Summer 1955), 340–350.

[3] *Go Down, Moses* (New York: Modern Library, 1955); page references are to this edition.

of jealous brooding had driven a hot iron into Lucas' pride. The next night he went to the white man's house to kill his kinsman. They had once lived as brothers: "they had fished and hunted together, they had learned to swim in the same water, they had eaten at the same table in the white boy's kitchen and in the cabin of the negro's mother; they had slept under the same blanket before a fire in the woods" (p. 55). But that was long ago. Now Lucas was protesting against the white man's prerogative over the black man's wife. That he was wrong in his suspicions is beside the point. He had to protest in order to assert the manhood that Southern heritage denied the Negro.

The fire in the hearth which Lucas had lit on his wedding day in 1895 "was to burn on the hearth until neither he nor Molly were left to feed it" (p. 47). This fire is symbolic of love. It is not the kind of love that Faulkner treated in *The Wild Palms* or *The Hamlet;* it is more akin to the warm affection that bound the MacCallum family together in *Sartoris.* In *Sartoris* that love was associated with life; its absence, as illustrated in Bayard's self-destructive course, with death. In "The Fire and the Hearth" love is threatened and invaded by the inherited curse which separates black from white.

The "old curse" (p. 111) descended too upon the next generation—on Roth, the son of Zack, and Henry, the son of Lucas. For seven years the boys had played together, eaten together, and slept together—the white boy even preferring the Negro cabin with its ever-burning fire—until one night the white boy had insisted that Henry sleep separately in the pallet below the bed. That night the white boy lay "in a rigid fury of the grief he could not explain, the shame he would not admit" (p. 112). They never slept again in the same room nor ate at the same table. The price for white supremacy was shame and loss of love.

Both as a boy and man, Roth Edmonds is characterized by the deprivation of love. The only mother he had ever known was the little Negress, Molly. It was she

> who had raised him, fed him from her own breast as she was actually doing her own child, who had surrounded him always with care for his physical body and for his spirit too, teaching him his manners, behavior—to be gentle with his inferiors, honorable with his equals, generous to the weak and considerate of the aged, courteous, truthful and brave to all—who had given him, the motherless, without stint or expectation of reward that constant and abiding devotion and love which existed nowhere else in this world for him. (p. 117)

He had lived his early life in the Negro cabin where "a little fire always burned, centering the life in it, to his own" (p. 110). Living as brother to Henry, he has wanted "only to love . . . and to be let alone" (p. 111). But that was his lost childhood which he had to forsake for the prerogatives of his Southern heritage. Southern heritage denied the black brother Roth's love and denied the white boy his brother's and mother's love. Faulkner's concern over this deprivation of love is not new, for "the tragic complexity of . . . motherless childhood" (pp. 130–131) echoes through Faulkner's novels. Many of his isolated and defeated protagonists —Quentin Compson, Joe Christmas, Joanna Burden, Gail Hightower, and Charles Bon—are marked by a motherless childhood. Behind the malaise and violence in Faulkner's works is the lost affection of childhood. But in *Go Down, Moses* the love that has been destroyed is the brotherhood between black and white.

The nostalgia for a lost love and innocence is central to "The Bear" too, although it has been enriched and transfigured in this story of the wilderness, since Faulkner has made use of a theme—a point of view, in fact—deeply embedded in American literature. In the conscious and unconscious memory of the American writer, the woods and river have loomed large because of their associations with a primitive and natural existence, free from the restraints and corruption of civilization. For Cooper the wilderness retained a primeval beauty and calm, though the simple, heroic Indians and Natty Bumppo had to yield to the destructive and possessive settlers. Based in part on the American frontier experience, the nostalgia for a primitive past seems to derive chiefly, however, from the author's own needs. This nostalgia often turns back to one's childhood—as if searching consciously for a lost innocence and freedom, and unconsciously for a lost peace. It is clearly evident in *Tom Sawyer* and *Huck Finn.* In *Tom Sawyer* the golden age of life is the carefree, joyous summertime of boyhood. In *Huck Finn* a boy and a slave, rafting down the friendly Mississippi, establish a brief idyll of peace and natural fellowship; but from the land come the representatives of civilization, armed with greed and deceit and violence, to shatter the idyll. The same opposition between nature and civilization, the same desire to retreat to an earlier, more natural way of life is apparent in "The Bear."

For the orphan Isaac McCaslin his true home would become the wilderness; his true father an old Indian who, quitting the plantation, returned to the wilderness whence he had derived. There as a self-appointed guardian of the woods Sam Fathers was to live out his remaining years. But already—it was 1877—the woods were "that doomed wilderness whose edges were being constantly and punily gnawed at by men with plows and axes who feared it because it was wilderness" (p. 193). In the face of its inevitable destruction, the old Indian trained the boy for initiation into the wilderness as though he were its priest and the boy the novitiate. But if Sam Fathers was the priest of the wilderness, Old Ben was its chief. To pass the ordeal of initiation the boy would have to win acceptance from the chief. To accomplish this the boy had to shed the instruments and symbols of civilization: the gun, watch, and compass. He had to conquer his fear, discipline his will, and, finally, like a humble suppliant before his god, surrender himself completely to the wilderness. The boy's communion was confirmed by the silent, mystical appearance of Old Ben.

Not long after the boy's initiation Sam Fathers found the dog who was brave enough, worthy enough to hunt the old bear. The dog possessed the hunter's fierce implacability—"the will and desire to pursue and kill . . . to endure beyond all imaginable limits of flesh in order to overtake and slay" (p. 237)—that had been "ordered and compelled by and within the wilderness" (pp. 191–192). This was the dog—they had named him Lion— who would be pitted against the bear in the last great hunt. These two kings of beasts seemed the sole surviving representatives of the ancient hunt and life of the wilderness. In the hunt that brooked no quarter, death was inevitable. The boy knew it, yet he did not hate Lion. "It seemed to him that there was a fatality in it. It seemed to him that something, he didn't know what, was beginning; had already begun. It was like the last act on a set stage. It was the beginning of the end of something" (p. 226). Despite these apprehensions he did not fully realize that the death of Old Ben signified the impending death of the wilderness. But Sam knew it. When Old Ben went down, "as a tree falls" (p. 241), "the old man, the wild man not even one generation from the woods, childless, kinless, peopleless" (p. 246) prepared to die too.

Joining Lion in its attack upon the bear was the halfbreed Indian, Boon Hogganbeck, who followed the dog as if Lion were his totem and represented his almost forsaken Indian heritage. Boon's killing of Old Ben entitles him to glory, but it has involved him too in the white man's guilt in the destruction of the woods. Boon served Major de Spain and McCaslin Edmonds. It was men like these who were destroying the wilderness—the Major by selling the woods to the lumber interests, McCaslin by clearing its borders in order to build farms and fill his bank's coffers. Great hunter for the moment, Boon was also an unwitting instrument of the wilderness' destruction. Of this the boy was dimly aware;

hence he stood apart from the action of the hunt, as if his will to act were paralyzed by his conflicting identification with both the hunted and the hunter. The ambivalence of the boy is embedded in the story itself, so that though "The Bear" celebrates the glory of the hunt, it mourns elegiacally the passing of the wilderness.

Implicit in the story is the dream of the wilderness as idyllic retreat, as an escape from the outside world to a reassuring but solitary peace. Like the river in *Huck Finn,* the woods in "The Bear" represents a retreat for a boy and a man, and like the river's idyll it was doomed to extinction by civilization. For Isaac McCaslin the woods came, more and more, to signify escape from woman, from the world and struggle. The figures to whom he surrendered, Old Ben and Sam Fathers, were solitary old bachelors identified with the wilderness. It was the wilderness that he embraced, the land that he repudiated. He had to repudiate, he explained to his cousin McCaslin Edmonds, because the land that did not belong to his father or grandfather or even Ikkemotubbe could not be bequeathed to him.

> Because He told in the Book how He created the earth, made it and looked at it and said it was all right, and then He made man. He made the earth first and peopled it with dumb creatures, and then He created man to be His overseer on the earth and to hold suzerainty over the earth and the animals on it in His name, not to hold for himself and his descendants inviolable title forever, generation after generation, to the oblongs and squares of the earth, but to hold the earth mutual and intact in the communal anonymity of brotherhood. (p.257)

For Isaac the golden age was the wilderness time when men lived as brothers before they had become tainted by the greed for possession. This primitivistic communism is not a new idea in Faulkner's works. In "Lo" (1935) an Indian reminded the President that "God's forest and the deer which He put in it belong to all"; in Thomas Sutpen's mountain home "the land belonged to anybody and everybody"; in "Retreat" (1938) Buck and Buddy McCaslin believed that "land did not belong to people but that people belonged to land." But it remained for Isaac McCaslin to develop this idea into a philosophy for life.[4] This

[4] Despite the relationship of this philosophy to the Indian and frontier point of view, the philosophy may stem from Rousseau's "Discourse on Inequality." Rousseau wrote: "The first man, who, after enclosing a piece of ground, took it into his head to say, 'This is mine,' and found people simple enough to believe him, was the true founder of civil society. How many crimes, how many wars, how many

philosophy ran absolutely counter to that of his ancestor, old Carothers. Carothers "took the land, got the land no matter how, held it to bequeath, no matter how, out of the old grant, the first patent, when it was a wilderness of wild beasts and wilder men, and cleared it, translated it into something to bequeath to his children, worthy of bequeathment for his descendants' ease and security and pride and to perpetuate his name and accomplishments" (p. 256). All that old Carothers represented Isaac was repudiating.

However, that he repudiated out of his belief in God's communistic scheme seems a rationalization of a more deeply rooted motive. He was driven to repudiation by the guilt inherited from the McCaslin sin against the Negro, a sin that had long since tainted the land. He first became aware of this sin when he was a boy of sixteen. In the "rank chill midnight room" (p. 271) of the McCaslin commissary he pored over the entries on the yellowed pages of the old ledgers. He was learning about his black kin: Eunice, who drowned herself in the creek on Christmas Day, 1832; Tomey, her daughter, who died in childbirth six months later; and the son Terrel, who was born in Tomey's death. Tomey's Terrel had been marked down in the old Carothers' will for a thousand dollar legacy. Yes, Isaac thought, his grandfather had found it cheaper to give a thousand dollars than to say "My son to a nigger" (p. 269). And Isaac thought of the young girl, Tomey: had there been any love between the old man and her, or had it been "just an afternoon's or a night's spittoon" (p. 270)? Suddenly he realized the truth: his grandfather had taken not only his slave but also "his own daughter" (p. 270). He knew now why Eunice had drowned herself. He saw that the McCaslin chronicle "was a whole land in miniature, which multiplied and compounded was the entire South" (p. 293), the "whole edifice . . . founded upon injustice and erected by ruthless rapacity and carried on even yet with at times downright savagery" (p. 298). The Southern planters "were all Grandfather" (p. 283). They had denied the heart's rights to their black kin; they had sold themselves to rapacity. Where were the "humility and pity and sufferance and pride of one to another" (p. 258) upon which

murders, how many misfortunes and horrors, would that man have saved the human species, who pulling up the stakes or filling up the ditches should have cried to his fellows: Be sure not to listen to this imposter; you are lost, if you forget that the fruits of the earth belong equally to us all, and the earth itself to nobody!" Compare Faulkner's remark in *Absalom, Absalom!* (Modern Library, p. 221): "Where he [the boy Thomas Sutpen] lived the land belonged to anybody and everybody and so the man who would go to the trouble and work to fence off a piece of it and say 'This is mine' was crazy."

God had founded and granted the new world to man? These virtues were part of the dream to which Isaac clung desperately in the face of his knowledge of the South's miscegenation and incest.

In Faulkner's novels incest tragically complicates the lives of his heroes and forces them to decisions that determine the course of their own and their descendants' lives. Quentin Compson yielded to the incestuous attraction of his sister Caddy; the result was his death by suicide. Charles Bon decided to marry his white sister; the result was his death by murder. Bayard Sartoris ("An Odor of Verbena") resisted his stepmother's offer of herself; the result was life and increased moral strength. Old Carothers took his slavedaughter Tomey; the result was the sin that oppressed his descendants' conscience. Incest and miscegenation are deeply rooted in the Southern past; they have evolved from the white planter's freedom with his woman slaves and have produced his double family—black and white. The white planter and his offspring were enmeshed in tragic conflicts and contradictions. On one hand, the South, with its emphasis upon family and honor, promoted strong familial bonds and obligations; on the other hand, the South refused to accord family status and love to a white man's black offspring. The black man's life was tragically scarred; the white man's conscience was grievously burdened.

To make a life of their own the black grandchildren of old Carothers abandoned the plantation in the 1880's. Tennie's Jim vanished forever somewhere in Tennessee in December 1885; seven months later Fonsiba went off with an educated Negro; only Lucas stayed on the plantation. To fulfill his grandfather's will and to ease his own conscience, Isaac went in search of Fonsiba. He found her living with her scholar-husband in Midnight, Arkansas. They were living with their delusion of freedom in a cold and empty cabin on an unfenced piece of jungle land. For Isaac these Negroes who had abandoned the plantation to embrace freedom and education were dwelling in darkness and delusion, as well as misery and poverty. It was twenty-two years after the Emancipation Proclamation, and still they were not free.

Neither was Isaac free, even after his repudiation of the cursed land in 1889. He had to repudiate, he told his cousin McCaslin, "because I have got myself to have to live with for the rest of my life and all I want is peace to do it in" (p. 288). But there was no peace. At the same time that Isaac was seeking to atone for the inherited sin, he was paralyzingly aware of the futility of his repudiation. Underlying his noble words is a sense

of desperation and grieving helplessness. He cried out to Fonsiba's husband:

> Dont you see? This whole land, the whole South, is cursed, and
> all of us who derive from it, whom it ever suckled, white and black
> both, lie under the curse? Granted that my people brought the curse
> onto the land: maybe for that reason their descendants alone can—
> not resist it, not combat it—maybe just endure and outlast it until
> the curse is lifted. Then your peoples' turn will come because we
> have forfeited ours. But not now. Not yet. Dont you see? (p. 278)

To the question of how long the land would be cursed, Isaac
replied to McCaslin: "It will be long. . . . But it will be all right
because they [the Negroes] will endure" (p. 299). Isaac has
offered the Negro the consolation that the Negro will endure, and
the blind faith that the wrong will be righted if one does nothing
long enough.

Yet this defeatism is not the true measure of Isaac McCaslin;
it is but the partial response of an embattled and struggling spirit.
Isaac, like the story itself, is torn in two by opposing forces.
One force moves him to atone for the sin against the Negro; the
other pushes him toward escape from the Southern dilemma. To
atone for the sin, he repudiated the land; but this proved to be
only a lonely gesture of the conscience that did not touch the
hard face of the world. To escape the dilemma he sought refuge
in the wilderness, where "he would be able to hide himself"
(p. 318). Like its protagonist, "The Bear" both retreats from and
confronts life. When it retreats from the Southern situation, it
tells beautifully and mystically of the hunt and the wilderness,
as though chanting an elegy for the passing of a golden age. When
the story confronts the Southern dilemma, it loses focus and
disintegrates. This is most apparent in the fourth section of the
story, which rambles from Isaac's discursive introversions to the
ledger entries to various uncorrelated episodes and finally to the
intrusive opinions of the author about the relative merits of the
South and the North. Both the protagonist and the author seem
to be battling with themselves—not in the manner of the author
of *Absalom, Absalom!* or *The Sound and the Fury* with its fine
controlled tension, but in the manner of one who is being frag-
mentized by unbearable guilt. It is not just the South's obsessional
guilt about the Negro, but it is the guilt implicit in a public admission of sin—a treasonable act for a Southerner.

By shifting the story's focus from the Negro to the wilderness, Faulkner is shifting the burden of guilt from the South to
mankind. It is mankind that, driven by rapacity, has destroyed

God's wilderness and enslaved His black creatures. Although the exploitation of nature is not morally the same as the enslavement of one's fellow man, Faulkner has chosen to merge these two crimes, as if to blur their moral distinctions. By fashioning a primitivistic mystique, with Christian overtones, based on God's will and the concept of the virgin wilderness as the golden age, Faulkner has endeavored to bulwark Isaac's conscience against the inroads of guilt. But this mystique is shot through with contradictions and weakness. On one hand, Faulkner has identified the wilderness with peace, brotherhood, pity, and humility; on the other hand, he has identified it with the primitive hunt that epitomizes "the will and desire to pursue and kill" (p. 237). Although the wilderness serves Isaac, as the seminary served Gail Hightower, as the temple of God, it serves also as a refuge from the world.

But there is no refuge from "the old wrong and shame" (p. 351). This is made apparent in the last two stories of the volume, "Delta Autumn" and "Go Down, Moses." Half a century has passed; the year is 1940 now. Time was running out for both Isaac and the wilderness. The diminishing wilderness had retreated toward the Delta; it had been replaced by the plumb-ruled highways, the tremendous gins, and the "ruthless mile-wide parallelograms" (p. 342) "of rank cotton for the frantic old-world people to turn into shells to shoot at one another" (p. 354). Although Uncle Ike saw the advancing destruction of the woods, he seemed sustained by a benign peace, a peace bought by his repudiation of the land. Uncle Ike's gentle, Christlike peace[5] is set against signs of vague unrest and ill omen: the remote European war; the faint light and dying warmth of the tent under the constant murmuring of the rain; the sullen brooding and harsh remarks of his kinsman and present owner of the McCaslin land, Roth Edmonds; and Will Legate's taunts about Roth's hunting of does.

The next morning Uncle Ike saw the doe. The doe was a young woman who had come in search of Roth. She was the mulatto granddaughter of Tennie's Jim, Old Carothers' Negro grandson. Unwittingly Roth Edmonds had committed miscegenation compounded by incest, his ancestor's sin. To this woman, his own black kin, Uncle Ike cried "in that thin not loud and grieving voice: 'Get out of here! I can do nothing for you! Cant nobody do nothing for you!'" (p. 361) His child's peace had been shattered. With quiet candor the mulatto woman reminded the shaking old

---

[5] Throughout the story, "Delta Autumn," Uncle Ike is frequently (eight times) described as peaceful and untroubled. Three times he is described with his hands crossed over his breast, three times compared to a gentle child.

man of a truth older than peace: "'Have you lived so long and forgotten so much that you don't remember anything you ever knew or felt or even heard about love?'" (p. 363) He was left with the wafting light and "grieving rain" (p. 365) and his shivering body and panting breath.

No Southerner can purchase immunity. Even for an Uncle Ike there is no peace in our time. The "old wrong and shame" has not been erased, but crops up anew in different guises. Now it is the South's honor and code that deny a woman's love; now it is the North's law that executes a Negro murderer for an aborted rebellion against the white society which has rejected him—the subject of the story "Go Down, Moses." The old Negress, Aunt Mollie, is ultimately right in her lament that Roth Edmonds sold her Benjamin to Pharaoh. The execution of Butch Beauchamp began long ago with the enslavement of the Negro by the Carothers McCaslins. Now, in the twentieth century, there is still no Moses, Faulkner says, to lead the Negro out of bondage.

Go Down, Moses voices the concern of conscience over the Negro's plight in a white man's world, yet it voices too the grief of conscience over its own helplessness. The South that denies the Negro his manhood denies the white man his right to love. The power of love cannot break through the world's hard shell. Isaac McCaslin's lonely act of atonement leaves no perceptible mark upon the Southern system. As the wilderness of the old Mississippi gives way to the fields of "rank cotton for the frantic old-world people to turn into shells to shoot at one another," it becomes apparent that the evil of the old world persists in the new. There is no peace. There is only the anguish of an old man to testify to the presence of the human conscience.

Bibliography

WORKS BY FAULKNER

Editions

The Marble Faun. Boston: Four Seas Co., 1924. Poems
Soldier's Pay. New York: Boni and Liveright, 1926. Novel
Mosquitoes. New York: Boni and Liveright, 1927. Novel
Sartoris. New York: Harcourt, Brace, 1929. Novel
The Sound and the Fury. New York: Jonathan Cape and Harrison Smith, 1929, Novel.
As I Lay Dying. New York: Jonathan Cape and Harrison Smith, 1930. Novel.
Sanctuary. New York: Jonathan Cape and Harrison Smith, 1931. Novel.
These Thirteen. New York: Jonathan Cape and Harrison Smith, 1931. Stories.
Light in August. New York: Harrison Smith and Robert Haas, 1932. Novel.
A Green Bough. New York: Harrison Smith and Robert Haas, 1933. Poems.
Doctor Martino and Other Stories. New York: Harrison Smith and Robert Haas, 1934. Stories.
Pylon. New York: Harrison Smith and Robert Haas, 1935. Novel.
Absalom, Absalom! New York: Random House, 1936. Novel.
The Unvanquished. New York: Random House, 1938. Novel.
The Wild Palms. New York: Random House, 1939. Novel.
The Hamlet. New York: Random House, 1940. Novel.
Go Down, Moses and Other Stories. New York: Random House, 1942. Novel; later entitled *Go Down, Moses* (New York: Modern Library, 1955).
Intruder in the Dust. New York: Random House, 1948. Novel.
Knight's Gambit. New York: Random House, 1949. Stories.
Collected Stories of William Faulkner. New York: Random House, 1950. Stories.
Requiem for a Nun. New York: Random House, 1951. Novel.
A Fable. New York: Random House, 1954. Novel.

Big Woods. New York: Random House, 1955. Stories.
The Town. New York: Random House, 1957. Novel.
The Mansion. New York: Random House, 1959. Novel.
The Reivers. New York: Random House, 1962. Novel.

Collections

Essays, Speeches, and Public Letters. Edited by James B. Meri-
  wether. New York: Random House, 1965.
The Faulkner Reader. New York: Random House, 1954.
The Portable Faulkner. Edited by Malcolm Cowley. Rev. ed. New
  York: Viking Press, 1967. First published in 1946. A section
  of Cowley's introduction is reprinted in this book (pp. 15–19).
Selected Short Stories of William Faulkner. New York: Modern
  Library, 1962.
William Faulkner. Edited by Eric Mottram. London: Routledge
  and Kegan Paul, 1971.
William Faulkner: Early Prose and Poetry. Edited by Carvel Col-
  lins. Boston: Little, Brown, 1962.
William Faulkner: New Orleans Sketches. Edited by Carvel Col-
  lins. Rev. ed. New York: Random House, 1968 (Grove Press
  edition, 1961).

BIBLIOGRAPHIES

Of Faulkner's Work

Massey, Linton R., comp. *William Faulkner: "Man Working,"*
  1919–1962: A Catalogue of the William Faulkner Collections
  at the University of Virginia. Introduction by John Cook
  Wyllie. Bibliographical Society of the University of Virginia,
  1968. A catalogue of the most complete collection of material
  by and about Faulkner now existing.
Meriwether, James B. *The Literary Career of William Faulkner:*
  A Bibliographical Study. Princeton: Princeton University
  Library, 1961. A description of materials in the Faulkner
  exhibition at the Princeton Library in 1957 with supplemen-
  tary sections.
———."William Faulkner: A Check List." *Princeton University*
  Library Chronicle 18 (Spring 1957): 136–58. Lists novels,
  stories, and other publications.

Of works about Faulkner

Beebe, Maurice. "Criticism of William Faulkner: A Selected
  Checklist." *Modern Fiction Studies* 13 (Spring 1967): 115–61.

Meriwether, James B. "William Faulkner." In *Fifteen Modern American Authors,* edited by Jackson R. Bryer, pp. 175–210. Durham, N.C.: Duke University Press, 1969.

Vickery, Olga W. "A Selective Bibliography." In *William Faulkner: Three Decades of Criticism,* edited by Frederick J. Hoffman and Olga W. Vickery, pp. 393–428. New York: Harcourt, Brace, 1963.

INTERVIEWS AND REMINISCENCES

Cowley, Malcolm. *The Faulkner-Cowley File: Letters and Memories, 1944–1962.* New York: Viking Press, 1966. The author's account of his relationship with Faulkner, and their correspondence.

Cullen, John B., in collaboration with Watkins, Floyd C. *Old Times in the Faulkner Country.* Chapel Hill: University of North Carolina Press, 1961. A fellow townsman and hunting companion relates his impressions of Faulkner, the fiction, and its possible sources.

Fant, Joseph L., III, and Ashley, Robert, eds. *Faulkner at West Point.* New York: Random House, 1964. Transcript of reading and interviews at the United States Military Academy in the spring of 1962, his last public appearance.

Falkner, Murry C. *The Falkners of Mississippi: A Memoir.* Baton Rouge: Louisiana State University Press, 1967. A family portrayal by the second Falkner son.

Faulkner, John. *My Brother Bill: An Affectionate Reminiscence.* New York: Trident Press, 1963 (Pocket Cardinal edition, 1964). A reminiscence of the novelist by the third of the four brothers.

Gwynn, Frederick L., and Blotner, Joseph L., eds. *Faulkner in the University: Class Conferences at the University of Virginia, 1957–58.* Charlottesville: University of Virginia Press, 1959 (reprinted by Vintage Books). Transcripts of discussions made while Faulkner was writer-in-residence at the University of Virginia, mainly on his own work. Excerpts about *The Sound and The Fury* are reprinted here (pp. 88–90).

Jelliffe, Robert A., ed. *Faulkner at Nagano.* Tokyo: Kenkyusha, 1956. Interviews, addresses, and press reports from Faulkner's 1955 visit to Japan at the invitation of the U.S. Department of State.

Meriwether, James B., and Millgate, Michael, eds. *Lion in the Garden: Interviews with William Faulkner.* New York: Random

House, 1968. A collection of the most important interviews
with Faulkner from 1926 to 1962. Reproduces those from
Nagano, but not from the University of Virginia or West
Point.

Webb, James W., and Green, A. Wigfall, eds. *William Faulkner
of Oxford.* Baton Rouge: Louisiana State University Press,
1965. The editors have collected comments on Faulkner from
persons who knew him.

BOOKS ON FAULKNER'S WORK

Adams, Richard Perrill. *Faulkner: Myth and Motion.* Princeton:
Princeton University Press, 1968. An attempt to provide a
central critical hypothesis for Faulkner's work.

Backman, Melvin. *Faulkner: The Major Years.* Bloomington:
Indiana University Press, 1966. A close analysis of ten novels
written during Faulkner's major period, 1929–1942. One essay, originally published in *PMLA,* is reprinted in this book
(pp. 136–146). Recommended.

Beck, Warren. *Man in Motion: Faulkner's Trilogy.* Madison:
University of Wisconsin Press, 1961. An analysis of the Snopes
trilogy: *The Hamlet, The Town,* and *The Mansion.*

Blotner, Joseph, comp. *William Faulkner's Library: A Catalogue.*
Charlottesville: University of Virginia Press, 1964. Lists the
books that Faulkner owned at the time of his death, with an
introduction.

Brooks, Cleanth. *William Faulkner: The Yoknapatawpha Country.* New Haven: Yale University Press, 1963. A thorough
account of the major novels set in Yoknapatawpha County
with three introductory chapters ("Faulkner the Provincial" is
reprinted in this volume, pp. 20–27), seventy-seven pages of
explanatory notes, six genealogical charts, and a character
index. Brooks has promised a subsequent study of Faulkner's
remaining work and his artistic development. Recommended.

Brylowski, Walter. *Faulkner's Olympian Laugh: Myth in the
Novels.* Detroit: Wayne State University Press, 1968. An examination of the mythical allusions and patterns in Faulkner's
fiction.

Coindreau, Maurice Edgar. *The Time of William Faulkner: A
French View of Modern American Fiction.* Edited and chiefly
translated by George McMillan Reeves, with a Foreword
by Michel Gresset. Columbia: University of South Carolina
Press, 1971. Essays and prefaces on contemporary American

literature by a French translator and critic, with eleven pieces on Faulkner.

Cowan, Michael, ed. *Twentieth Century Interpretations of "The Sound and The Fury": A Collection of Critical Essays.* Englewood Cliffs, N.J.: Prentice-Hall, 1968. Essays about Faulkner's novel of the Compson family.

Hoffman, Frederick J. *William Faulkner.* New York, Twayne, 1961. A general account of the work, stressing the major novels. Criticism of *The Sound and The Fury* is reprinted in this volume (pp. 77–87). Recommended.

Hoffman, Frederick J., and Vickery, Olga W., eds. *William Faulkner: Three Decades of Criticism.* New York: Harcourt, Brace, 1963. Paperback edition of Michigan State University Press book (1960). A thorough revision of the same editors' *Two Decades* with a long introduction and a 36-page bibliography. Recommended.

—— and ——, eds. *William Faulkner: Two Decades of Criticism.* East Lansing: Michigan State College Press, 1951. The first collection of critical essays.

Howe, Irving. *William Faulkner: A Critical Study.* 2d ed. New York: Vintage Books, 1962. Revision of critical book first published in 1952. Recommended.

Hunt, John W. *William Faulkner: Art in Theological Tension.* Syracuse: Syracuse University Press, 1965. Investigates the proposition that Faulkner "employs strategies implying a complex theological vision" with three central chapters on *The Sound and The Fury, Absolam, Absolam!* and "The Bear."

Kerr, Elizabeth M. *Yoknapatawpha: Faulkner's "Little Postage Stamp of Native Soil."* New York: Fordham University Press, 1969. Studies the relationship between the fictional Yoknapatawpha and the people, history, and geography of Faulkner's native Lafayette County, Mississippi.

Kirk, Robert W., with Klotz, Marvin. *Faulkner's People: A Complete Guide and Index to Characters in the Fiction of William Faulkner.* Berkeley: University of California Press, 1963. The characters are listed with page references under the novels and stories in which they appear. Recommended.

Langford, Gerald. *Faulkner's Revision of "Absalom, Absalom!": A Collation of the Manuscript and the Published Book.* Austin: University of Texas Press, 1971.

Langford, Gerald. *Faulkner's Revision of "Sanctuary": A Collation of the Manuscript and the Published Book.* Austin: University of Texas Press, 1972.

Longley, John Lewis, Jr. *The Tragic Mask: A Study of Faulkner's*

Heroes. Chapel Hill: University of North Carolina Press, 1963. The major characters analyzed for their comic and tragic qualities. "Thomas Sutpen: The Tragedy of Aspiration" is reprinted in this volume (pp. 110–121). Recommended.

Millgate, Michael. *The Achievement of William Faulkner.* New York: Random House, 1966. A critical review of the novels and short stories, opening with a 59-page biographical chapter. The chapter on *As I Lay Dying* is reprinted here (pp. 91–101). Recommended.

Minter, David L., ed. *Twentieth Century Interpretations of "Light in August": A Collection of Critical Essays.* Englewood Cliffs, N.J.: Prentice-Hall, 1969. Essays by various critics.

O'Connor, William Van. *The Tangled Fire of William Faulkner.* Minneapolis: The University of Minnesota Press, 1954. Criticism of the work through *Requiem for a Nun,* with biographical material. Recommended.

——— . *William Faulkner.* Minneapolis: University of Minnesota Press, 1959. A 43-page pamphlet on Faulkner's work and career.

Peavey, Charles D. *Go Slow Now: Faulkner and the Race Question.* Eugene: University of Oregon Books, 1971.

Richardson, H. Edward. *William Faulkner: The Journey to Self Discovery.* Columbia: University of Missouri Press, 1969. The early life and work through the publication of *Sartoris* (1929).

Slatoff, Walter Jacob. *Quest for Failure: A Study of William Faulkner.* Ithaca, N.Y.: Cornell University Press, 1960. A study advancing the thesis that Faulkner's work takes a paradoxical and ambiguous view of human experience.

Swiggart, Peter. *The Art of Faulkner's Novels.* Austin: University of Texas Press, 1962. A study of Faulkner's narrative techniques.

Thompson, Lawrance. *William Faulkner: An Introduction and Interpretation.* 2nd ed. New York: Holt, Rinehart, 1967. A critical interpretation of major novels. The chapter on *The Hamlet* is reprinted here (pp. 122–135). Recommended.

Tuck, Dorothy. *Apollo Handbook of Faulkner.* New York: Thomas Y. Crowell, 1969. Originally published in 1964, this handbook includes critical summaries of the fiction, a listing of characters, genealogical charts, and a chapter of biography.

Utley, Francis Lee; Bloom, Lynn Z.; and Kinney, Arthur F., eds. *Bear, Man, and God: Eight Approaches to William Faulkner's "The Bear."* 2d ed. New York: Random House, 1971.

A collection of background material and critical opinions on "The Bear."

Vickery, Olga W. *The Novels of William Faulkner: A Critical Interpretation.* Rev. ed. Baton Rouge: Louisiana State University Press, 1964. A critical examination of the themes and characters in the novels, first published in 1959 and revised after Faulkner's death. Final chapter is reprinted in this volume (pp. 28–44). Recommended.

Volpe, Edward L. *A Reader's Guide to William Faulkner.* New York: Farrar, Straus, 1964. This volume contains an introduction on Faulkner's life and literary characteristics, critical assessments of all the novels, chronologies of the seven most difficult narratives, seven genealogical tables including that of the Faulkner family, and a bibliography. The author is preparing another book on the short stories. Recommended.

Waggoner, Hyatt H. *William Faulkner: From Jefferson to the World.* Lexington: University of Kentucky Press, 1959. An examination of the novels and four short stories.

Warren, Robert Penn, ed. *Faulkner: A Collection of Critical Essays.* Englewood Cliffs, N.J.: Prentice-Hall, 1966. Selection of essays by various critics with an introduction by the editor (reprinted in this volume, pp. 58–76). Recommended.

Watson, James Gray. *The Snopes Dilemma: Faulkner's Trilogy.* Coral Gables, Fla.: University of Miami Press, 1970. A study of the Snopes family.

Catalog

If you are interested in a list of fine Paperback
books, covering a wide range of subjects
and interests, send your name and address,
requesting your free catalog, to:

McGraw-Hill Paperbacks
1221 Avenue of Americas
New York, N.Y. 10020